VIOLIN PRIMER
by
JIM TOLLES

HOW TO USE THE

If you are using the book and video together, follow these suggestions. The book can be used by itself if the video is not available.

Step 1
Watch a section of the video. Rewind and watch again until you understand it completely. (A section would be from one title page to the next).

Step 2
Once you understand the section, go to the book to practice the exercises and songs over and over until you are comfortable with them.

Step 3
After practicing with the book, go back to the video and play along with the video to make sure you are performing the material properly

This course is designed to be worked through, stopping and practicing each section until you are thoroughly familiar with it. It will probably take the average beginning student 2 - 4 months to work all the way through the book and video, so don't get in a hurry. Take your time and learn the material correctly.

DEDICATION

This book is dedicated to my students. All have helped me grow as a teacher, just as I hope I have helped them grow as violinists.

Copyright 1996 by Cassette & Video Learning Systems
ALL RIGHTS RESERVED. Any copying, arranging, or adapting of this work without the consent of the owner is an infringement of copyright.

INTRODUCTION

The Violin Primer is an instruction book with CD designed for the beginning student who desires a clear, step by step method of learning to play the violin or fiddle. Many illustrations are included to make this the easiest to understand course available. The book contains not only familiar songs, but spends much time showing techniques and exercises to help establish a firm foundation and background so necessary in learning to play any instrument.

The audio CD that accompanies this book will enable the student to learn 3 or 4 times faster than with other methods. This CD provides the accent, tone, and rhythm for all the songs and exercises in this book. In addition, if you have the *Introduction to Violin* video, you will be able to see the correct movements of the left and right hand.

THE AUTHOR

Jim Tolles has been playing violin and fiddle for 30 years and teaching for 25. He is an accomplished performer, having appeared with Goose Creek Symphony, Breakfast Special, touring Broadway shows, and numerous country and bluegrass bands native to his Atlanta, Georgia home. He is currently a full time teacher in Atlanta. Jim has recorded with various artists on the Capitol, Atteiram, and Rounder labels and has written songs on those labels as well as Flying Fish. Jim's playing has been featured on national radio and TV commercials. This course is a product of those 20 years of teaching and his desire to help the beginning player get off to the best possible start. Jim also wrote *The Fiddle Primer* book and *Introduction to Violin* video.

COMPANION VIDEO

The companion video, *Introduction to Violin*, is a valuable supplement to the Violin *Primer* course. The video shows the correct movement of both the left and right hands which can only be seen on screen. In addition, it covers the material in the book utilizing the latest in video technology (split screen, on screen tablature, state of the art graphics, special effects, and animation) to add further emphasis and clarity for the beginning student. This video is available at your local store or send $14.95 plus $4.00 shipping and handling to:

Cassette & Video Learning Systems
1882 Queens Way
Atlanta, GA 30341
800-416-7088

VIDEO COUNTER

The video counter is included in the Violin Primer book to show you where each lesson is located on the companion video. Check the counter number as it appears on screen in the video and then scan to the exact location you want

CD COUNTER

All of the material in the Violin Primer book is played on the CD. The CD Counter logo indicates the track number for each piece of music.

TABLE OF CONTENTS

	Book	CD 01	00:00
SECTION I - Getting Started			
Parts of the Violin & Bow	1	01	01:45
Shoulder Rest	2		02:00
Bow Preparation	3		02:25
Tuning	4	02	03:25
Holding The Violin	5		05:20
Left Hand Position	8		06:30
Left Arm Position	9		07:15
Holding The Bow	10		07:30
Bowing Open Strings	12		09:05
Music Notation	14		16:00
Open String Exercises	15	03-11	10:05
Noting The Violin	20	12-17	16:50
Our First Song	22	18	23:25
Here We Go	23	19	24:35
Mary Had A Little Lamb	24	20-23	25:05
G, A, & B Notes	26	24-27	26:30
The Alphabet Song	27	28-31	31:50
Practice	29		35:10
SECTION II - Playing			
Slurs	31	32-39	35:55
Go Tell Aunt Rhody	33	40	40:30
The D Scale	35	44-54	41:25
3/4 Time	38	55-58	46:50
Sunday Waltz	39	59	48:30
C Natural	40	62-64	
Jenny Pluck Pears	41	65	
Ties	42	67-68	
When The Saints Go Marching In	42	69	
Red River Valley	43	70	
Notes On The E String	43	71-82	
Seagulls And Seals	46	83-84	
Sweet On Violin	47	85-86	

SECTION 1
GETTING STARTED

PARTS OF THE VIOLIN AND BOW

- Wooden Friction Pegs
- Scroll
- Nut
- Fingerboard
- Strings
- Purfling
- Bridge
- F hole
- Fine Tuners
- Tailpiece
- Chin Rest
- Tail Pin
- Button or Screw

- Tip
- Hair
- Stick
- Frog

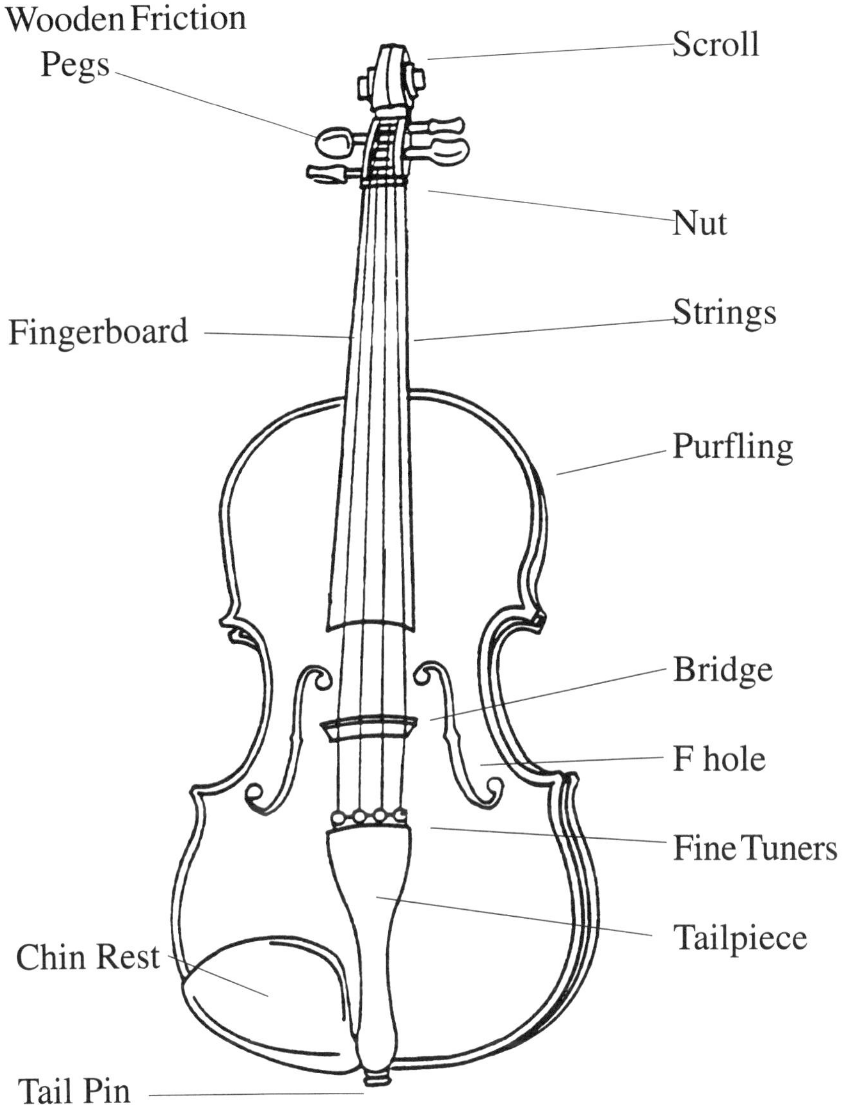

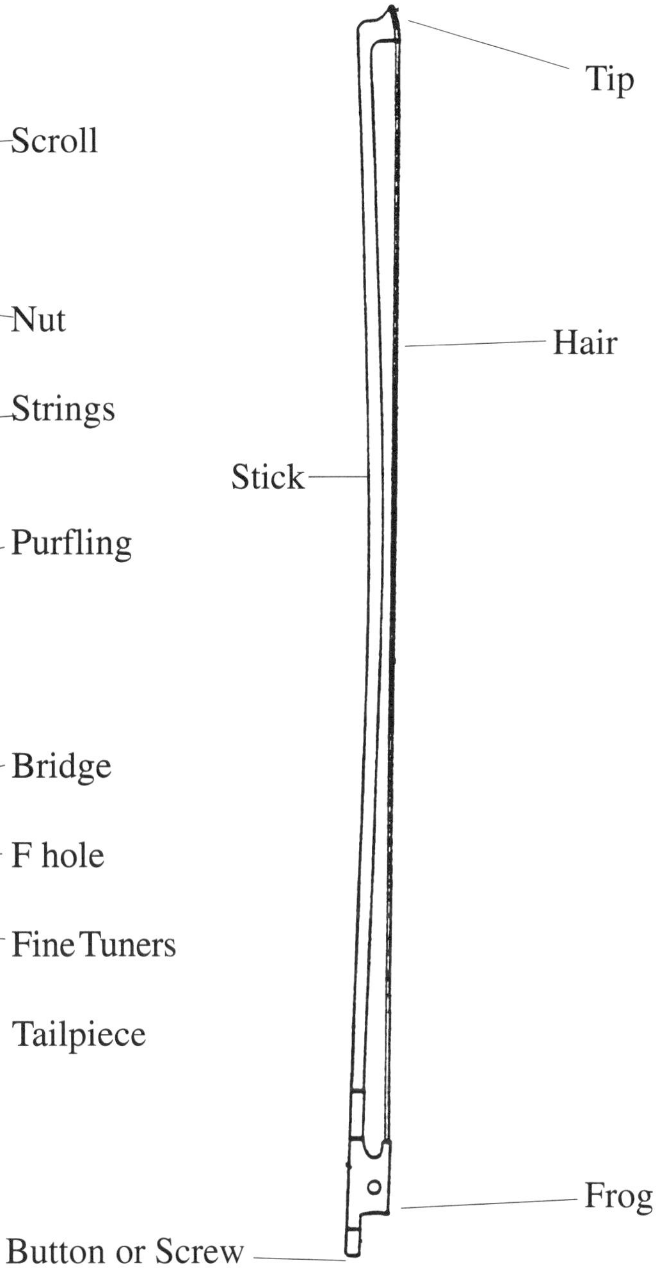

Take your violin and bow to your local music store to make sure they are in proper working order. See that the strings are in good condition and that the bow has enough hair and works properly. Also have them tune it for you.

If you are teaching yourself to play the violin without the aid of a teacher, we feel that using both the video and the book will make learning much easier. There are many details to holding the violin and bow, and using both teaching methods will enable you to learn proper techniques much faster.

SHOULDER REST

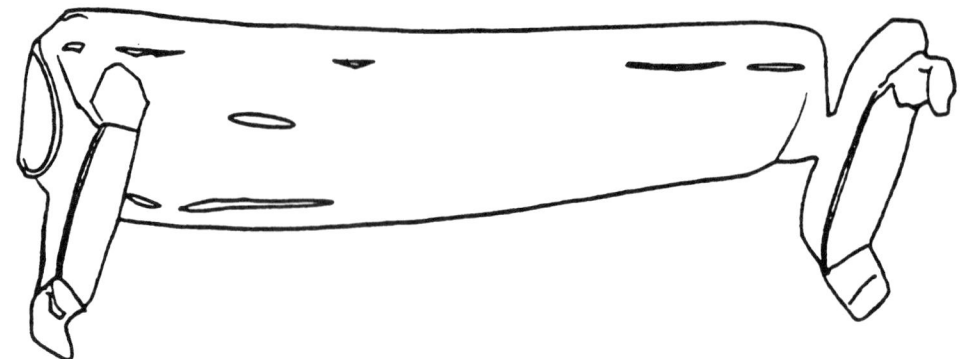

Get a shoulder rest that looks like this. There are several different kinds on the market and you may need to experiment, but we recommend this one.

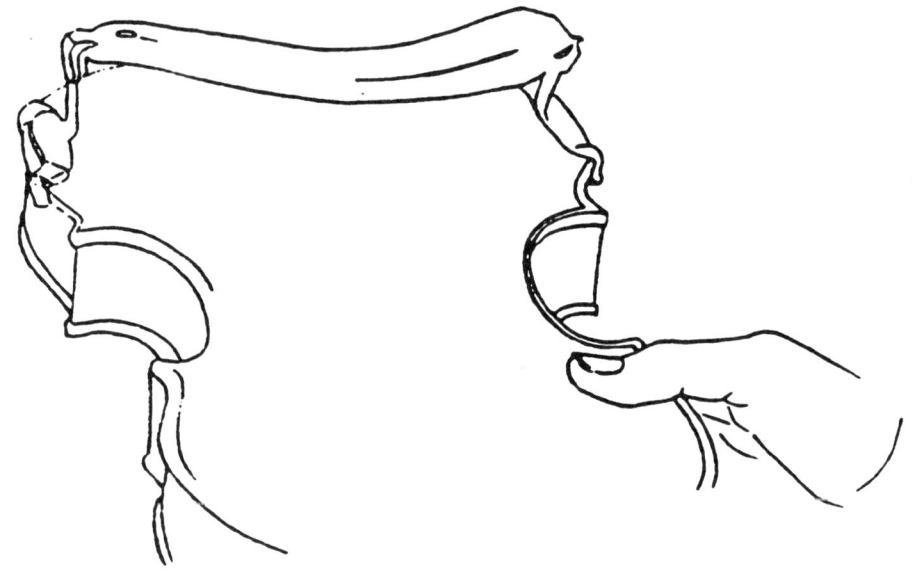

FINE TUNERS

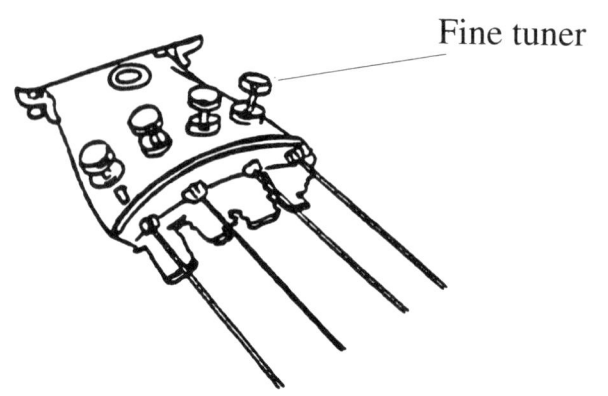

Fine tuner

Have fine tuners installed on the tailpiece. These are a necessity if you have steel strings on your violin. If you are playing on nylon strings, only one fine tuner is required for the E string or 1st string.

BOW PREPARATION

TIGHTENING & LOOSENING

Before playing, tighten the bow. Turn the screw clockwise so that the bow hair comes away from the stick, but not so much that you lose the curve of the bow. When you're finished playing, loosen the bow so that when you tap the stick, the bow hair just begins to flop.

ROSIN

Violinists & fiddlers play with different amounts of rosin. First, tighten the bow in order to apply rosin. Draw the bow back and forth against the rosin. Press hard and use short strokes. When you feel you have enough, use long strokes to distribute the rosin. If the bow just barely makes a sound on the strings, you need more rosin. If clouds of rosin come flying off as you play, you have too much rosin.

REHAIRING

Bow hairs do break and eventually you will need to have your bow rehaired. Have your bow checked to make sure it does not need to be rehaired.

Button or Screw

TUNING THE VIOLIN

You should tune the violin at the start of every practice session. The wooden friction pegs are used to make large changes in pitch (see page 1). The fine tuners make smaller changes. Bow the D or 3rd string. If it is a long way out of tune, pluck it and turn the friction peg. Then bow the string and simultaneously turn the fine tuner by reaching underneath the violin. At first you may need to take your violin to a music store or violin teacher for help.

AUDIO CD OR VIDEO TAPE

Listen to the CD to hear the correct pitch. Tune close to the correct pitch with the wooden friction pegs, then use the fine tuners to make it exact. Tune all four strings in this manner.

PIANO

If you have a piano or keyboard at home, it can be used as a tuning source. The following diagram shows which note on the piano matches each open string of the violin.

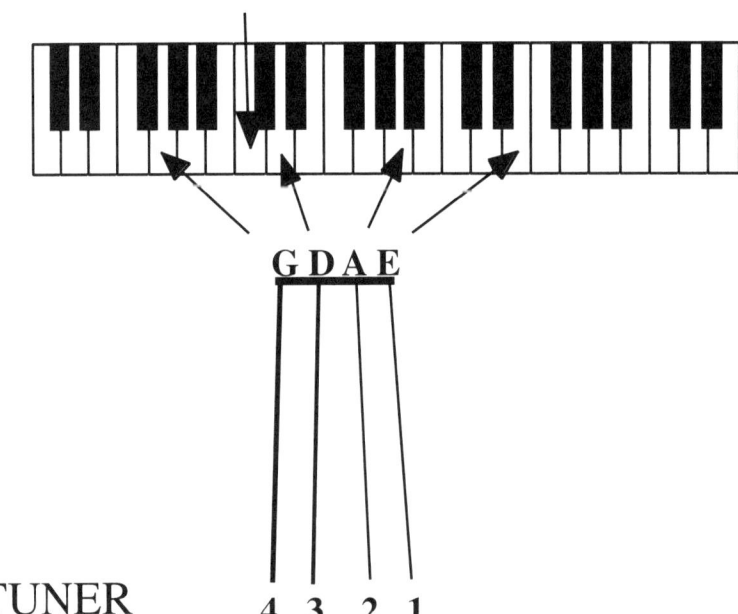

ELECTRONIC TUNER

I recommend that you purchase an electronic tuner as soon as possible. They cost about $30 - $50 at you local music store and will enable you to tune very easily. Most stores will be happy to show you how to use the tuner.

HOLDING THE VIOLIN

You can play the violin standing or sitting. Standing helps many folks get the feel of the instrument and avoids the problem of the bow hitting your leg while seated. We recommend that beginners practice standing up. Check the following diagrams.

Sitting

Standing

HOLDING THE VIOLIN

05:40

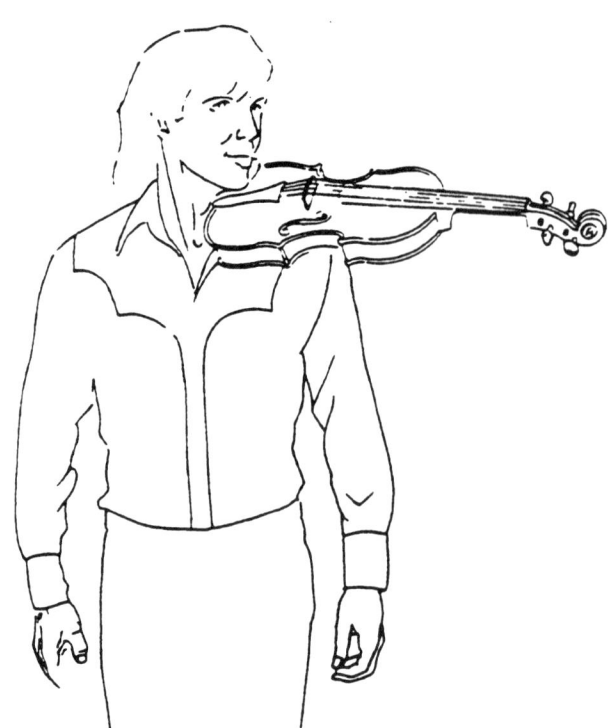

Put the violin under your chin and over your left collarbone. You should be able to support the violin without using your left hand. The chin rest is really a jaw bone rest. Turn your head so that it is halfway between straight ahead and looking down the violin.

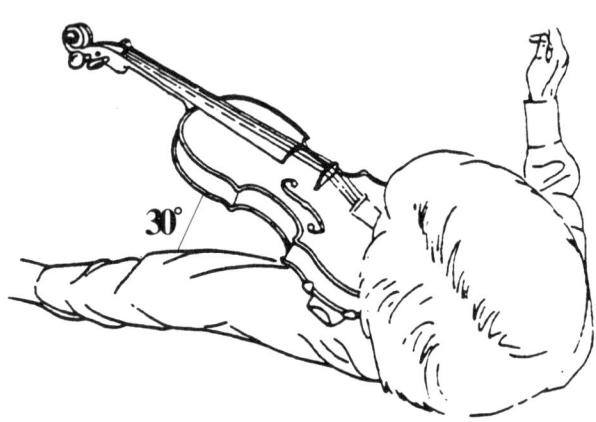

The violin should be at a thirty degree angle to the left arm.

The violin should be parallel to the floor, not tilted up or down.

HOLDING THE VIOLIN

The violin should have an easy slope towards the floor. The following diagram shows the correct angle.

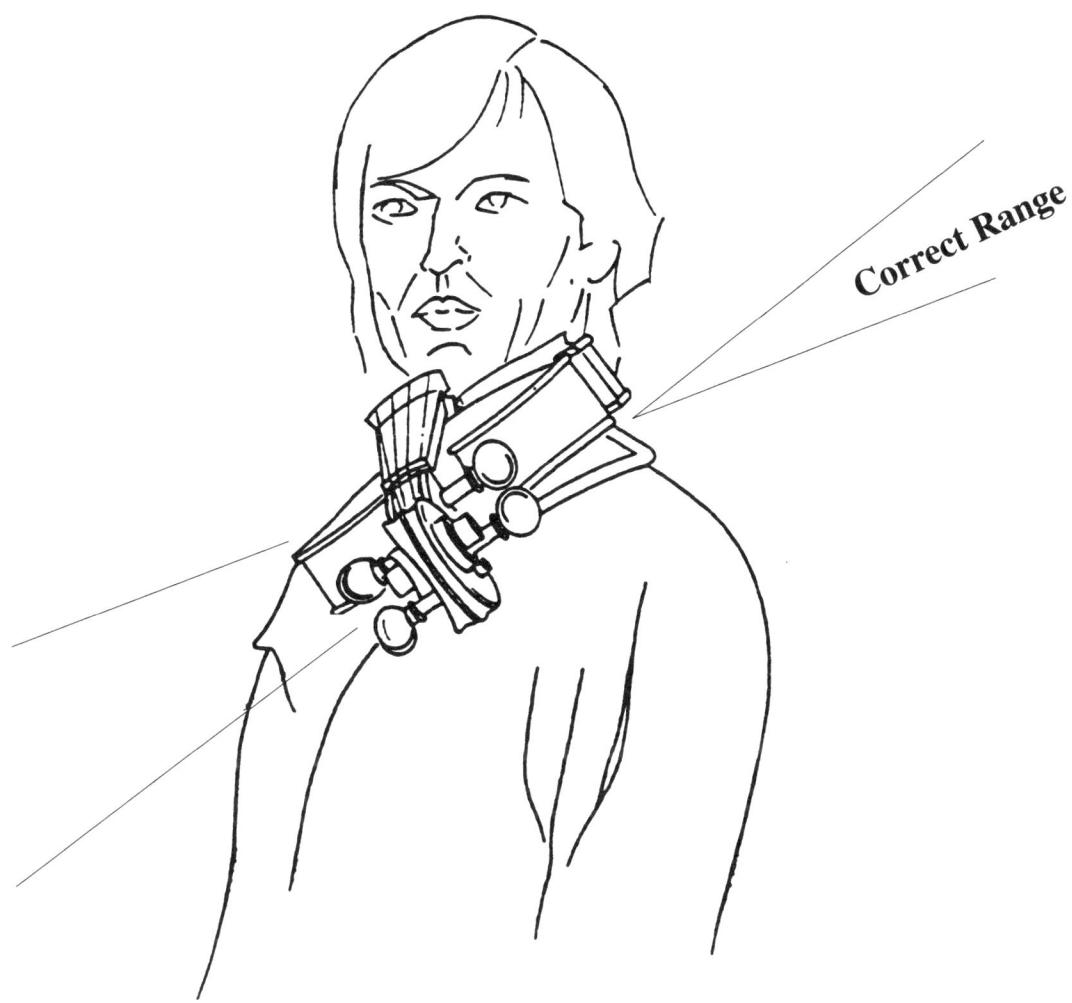

Stand in front of a mirror to compare yourself to the above diagram.

LEFT HAND POSITION

 06:30

Next we'll check your left hand to make sure you are holding the neck of the violin properly. Take the V that your thumb and forefinger make (Figure A) and close it so that the neck of the violin makes contact with your thumb, just above the first joint and the side of your hand on that bump where your forefinger joins on (Figure B).

This will create a small space below the neck. Don't let the neck of the violin fall into this space. Figure C shows the violin from the player's perspective.

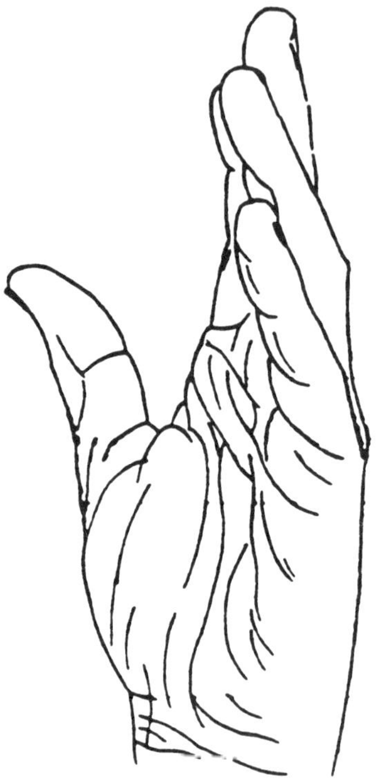

Figure A

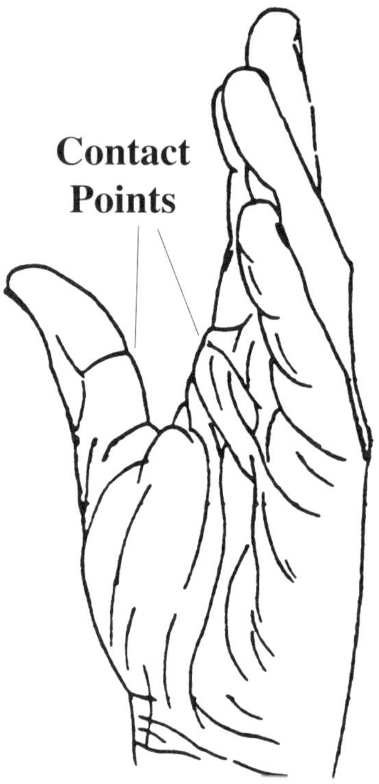

Figure B

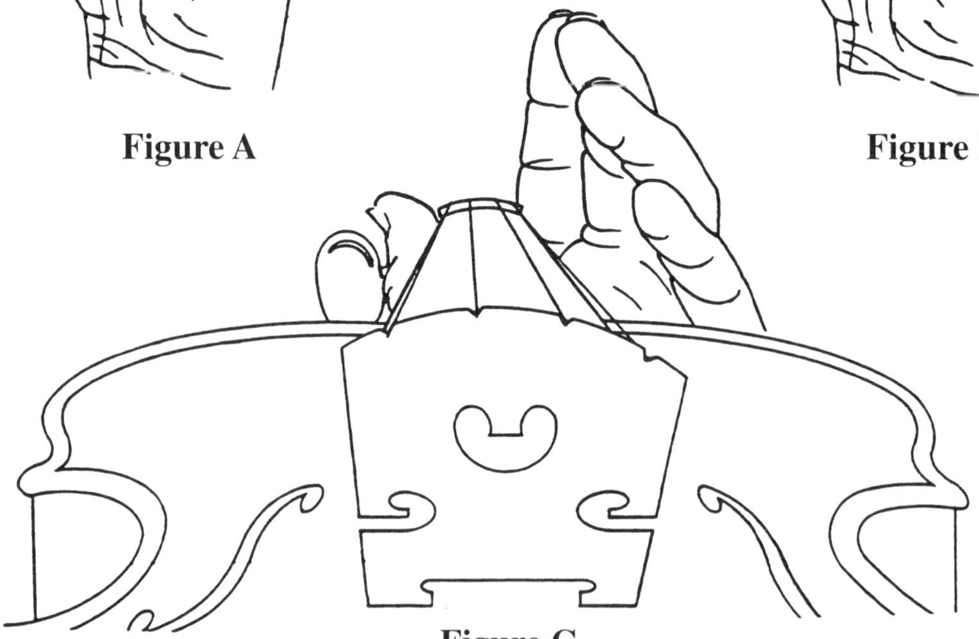

Contact Points

Figure C

8

LEFT ARM POSITION

The left elbow should be under the violin, as far as it will go, not out to the side as illustrated in the following diagrams.

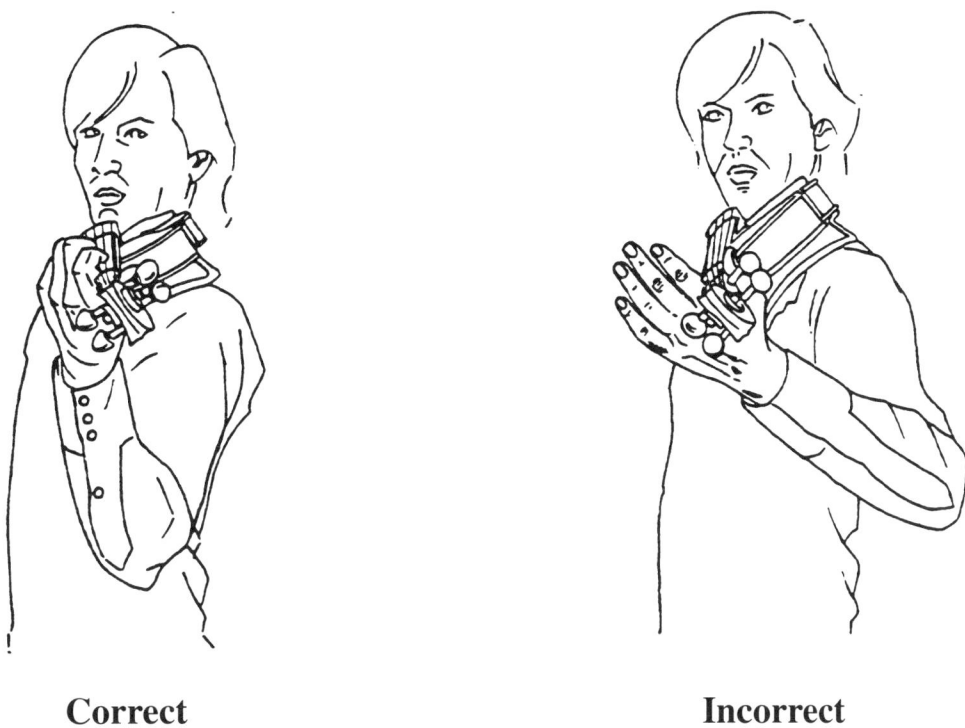

Correct   **Incorrect**

The wrist should be straight or bent slightly away from you. Do not let the wrist collapse or touch the rib of the instrument.

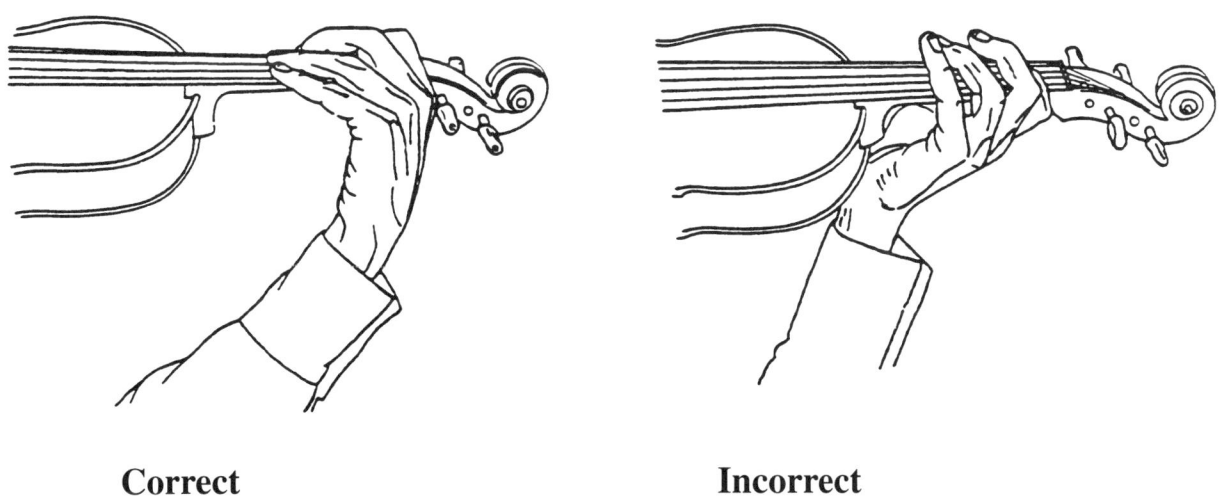

Correct   **Incorrect**

HOLDING THE BOW

Put the violin down so that you have both hands free to learn how to hold the bow. We will follow four steps:

1. Form a backwards C with the thumb and middle fingers of the right hand, bending the joint of the thumb as closely as possible to a right angle.

2. Now press the tip of your thumb into the middle joint of your middle and ring fingers. These are the primary points of contact.

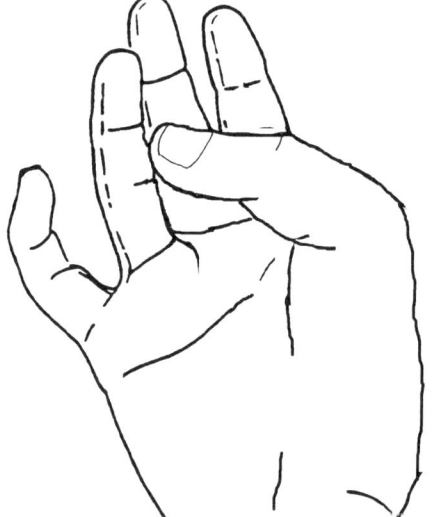

3. Holding the bow with your left hand, grasp the bow near the frog on the thumb leather. The index finger goes on at the first joint about 3/4 of an inch up the bow. The pinkie is arched and touches at the tip. The thumb touches the bow hair.

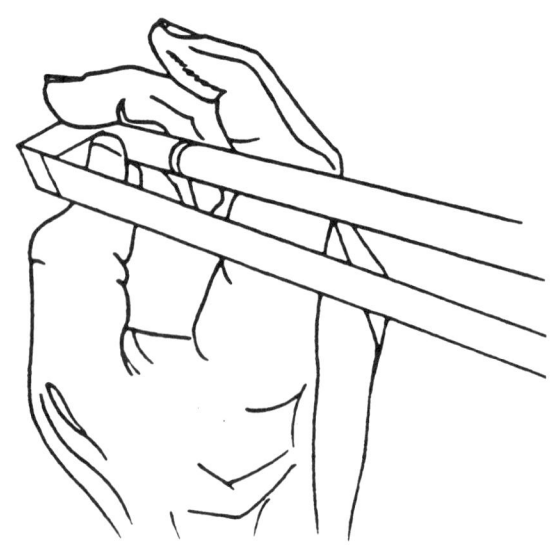

HOLDING THE BOW

4. At this point you may notice that your fingers are at right angles to the stick. Turn them so that they are at about a 45 degree angle. Now hold your hand in front of a mirror and compare it to the following diagrams (remember the thumb is still at a right angle).

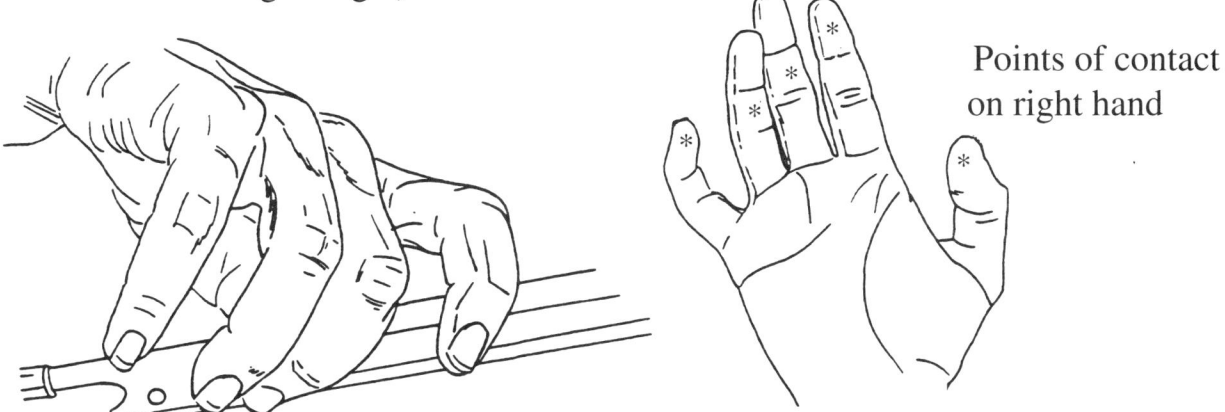

Points of contact on right hand

This bow grip may seem awkward so allow some time for the muscles in your hand to strengthen and stretch.

Pick up the violin and put it under your chin. The bow must be at right angles to the strings at all times. It can be difficult to look down at the bow and strings and tell just when you have a right angle.

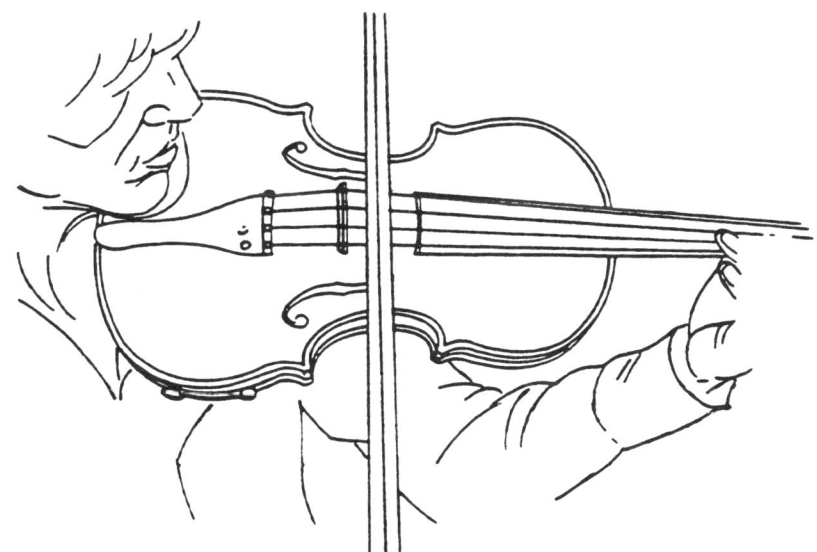

An easy solution is to stand in front of a mirror. Turn your body so that the neck of the violin is parallel to the mirror. Then turn your head in the chin rest and look in the mirror and it will be possible to make small corrections quite easily.

BOWING OPEN STRINGS

It is very important to be able to bow open strings correctly before trying to play melodies on the violin. An open string means one that is not being pressed down by a finger of the left hand.

The bow should strike the strings halfway between the bridge and the end of the fingerboard. The bow should travel across the strings at a right angle, not slanted in either direction.

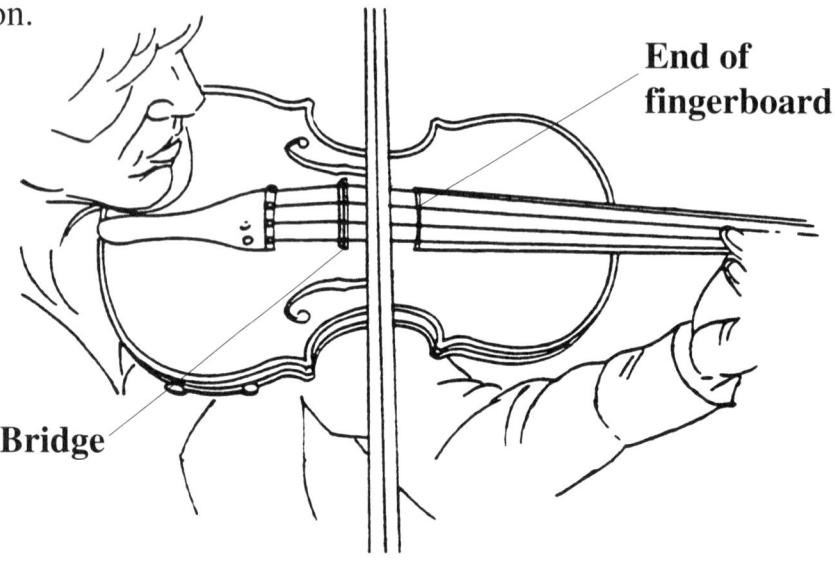

The action of the arm, if held stiffly, will cause the bow to move awkwardly, so use the shoulder, elbow, and wrist to make it go straight. Use plenty of fluid wrist action. When your right hand approaches the strings, your wrist should be bent upward. As it moves away, the wrist should bend downward as follows:

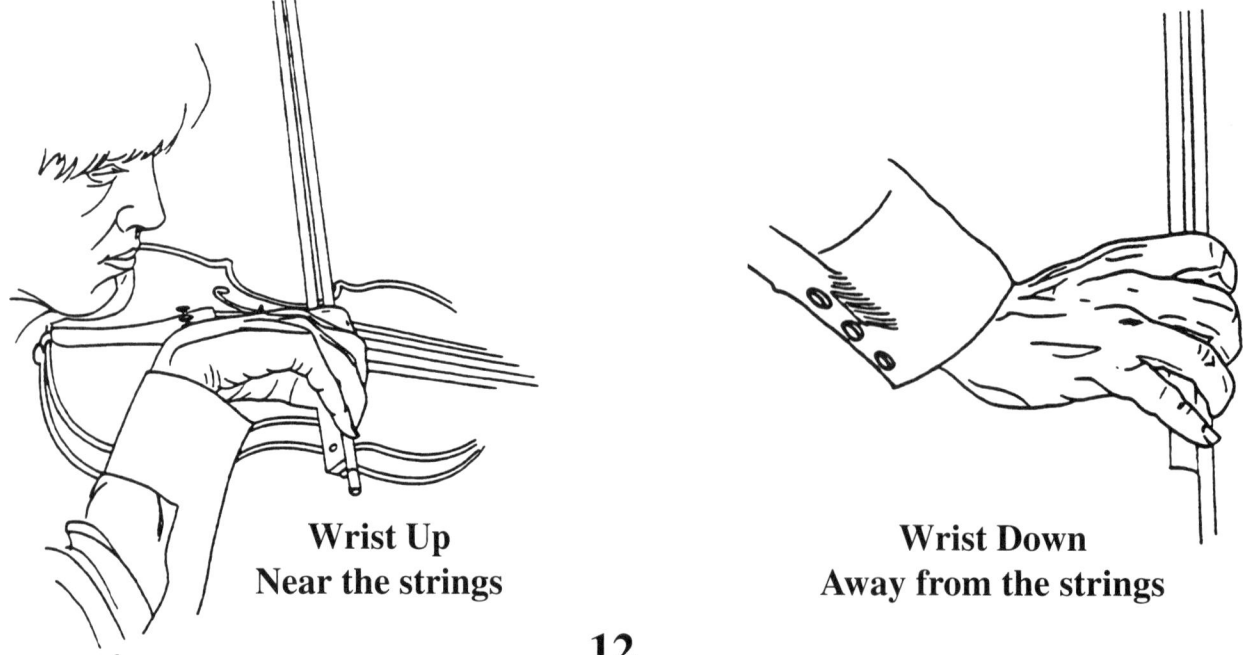

Wrist Up
Near the strings

Wrist Down
Away from the strings

BOWING OPEN STRINGS

The right elbow should be no higher than the bow. This will vary, depending on which string you are bowing.

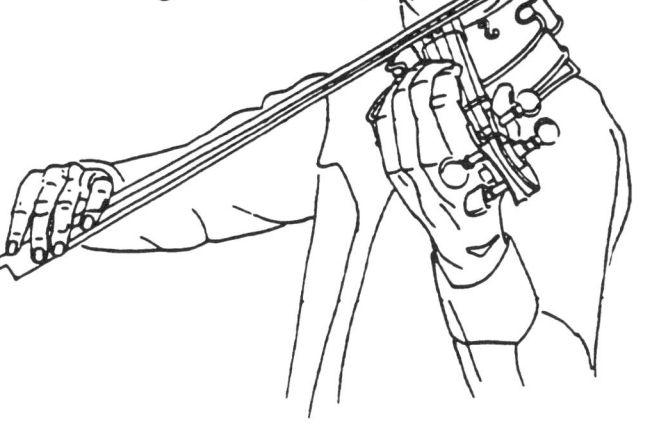

Correct

Incorrect

MUSIC NOTATION

As we begin to bow the strings, we'll gradually explain how to read music. The five horizontal lines are called the staff (see diagram below). At the extreme left of music written for violin, you will see the treble clef. Notes may be written on the lines or in spaces in between the lines. Higher pitches are written on physically higher positions on the staff. Lower notes on lower positions. The notes of our common major scale alternate space, line, space, line, etc. The pitch sounded by bowing the open 3rd string is D. It's location is in the space below the bottom line of the staff. This will be the 1st note of our scale. The next note in the scale is E, found on the bottom line.

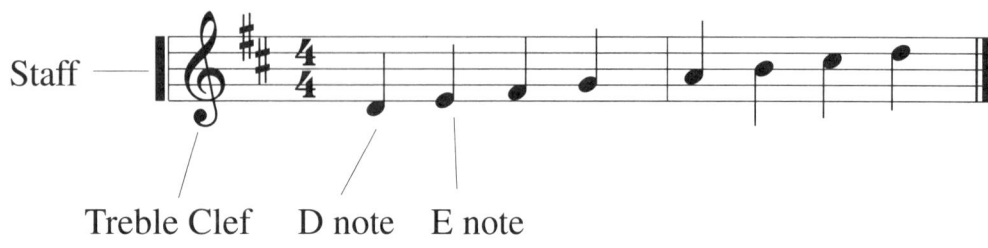

We'll introduce rhythm or meter right here. Reading left to right, the staff has bar lines every so often. The spaces between these lines are called bars or measures. Within each measure there is always the same number of pulses or beats. The time signature at the left tells us how many beats per measure. In the example here, we'll use 4/4 time. The top number tells us how many beats per measure. The bottom number tells us what kind of note receives 1 beat. In this case, the 4 on the bottom indicates a quarter note. A quarter note looks like this (♩). It has a solid head and a stem and receives 1 beat. We'll also need to know half notes. They have open heads and stems and receive 2 beats (♩). After playing all of the exercises in the following section along with the CD or video tape, you should have a clear understanding of musical notation.

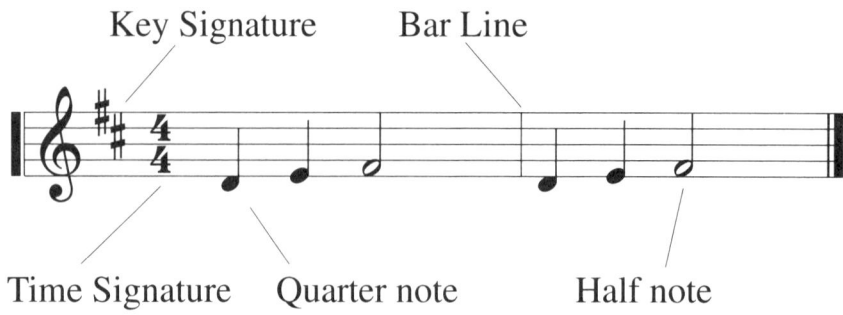

14

EXERCISE 1

10:05

Now we are ready to start bowing open strings. First check your bow grip. Next, place the hair of the bow on the 3rd string near the frog. Draw the bow out to the tip to a count of 4 (this is a down bow). Draw the bow back to the frog to a count of 4 (this is an up bow). There should be as little break in sound as possible between the down bow and the up bow. Try not to let the bow slow down at the end of the stroke and connect one note to another. Play along with the CD or video tape.

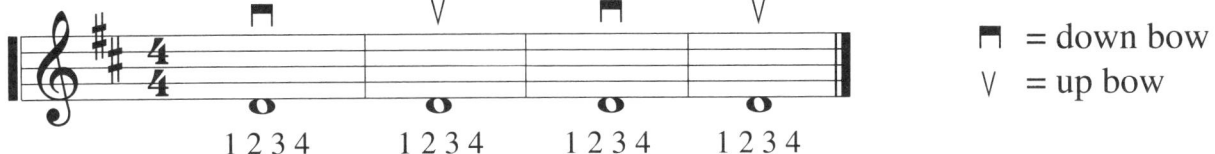

⊓ = down bow
V = up bow

Compare yourself to the video or practice in front of a mirror to make sure that you are using the proper technique.

EXERCISE 2

As we go from string to string, we must change the bow angle. The angle of the bow is critical to avoid hitting adjacent strings. Drop the angle of the bow down to play the 2nd string. Then play the same 4 count exercise on the 2nd string.

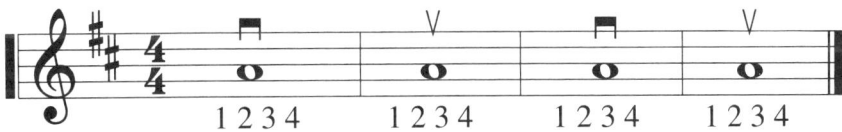

EXERCISE 3

Drop the angle of the bow even further for the 1st string.

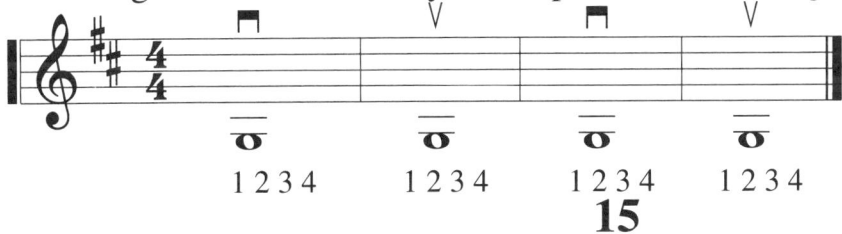

EXERCISE 4

Bring the bow all the way back up for the 4th string.

15

HALF NOTES

EXERCISE 5

Next we'll bow down and up to the count of 2, playing half notes. Put the bow on the 3rd string (D string) just below the middle. Draw it out to within a few inches of the tip and back to where you started. Count 1, 2 for the down bow and 3,4 for the up bow. Play along with the CD or video tape.

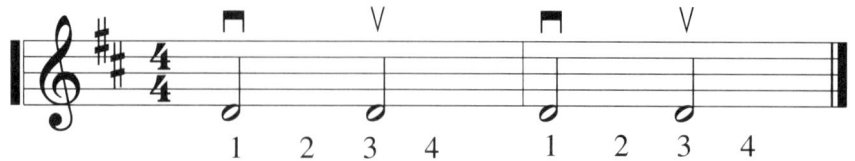

♩ = Half note

EXERCISE 6

Now for half notes on the 2nd string or A string.

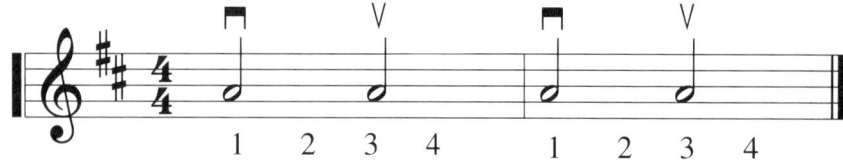

EXERCISE 7

Again, the same thing on the first string or E string.

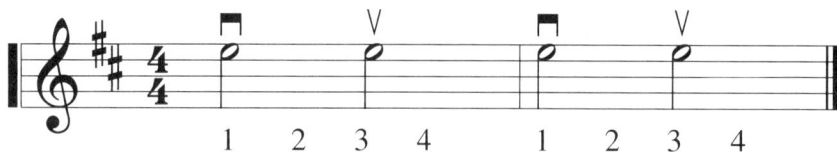

EXERCISE 8

Now back down to the 4th string or G string.

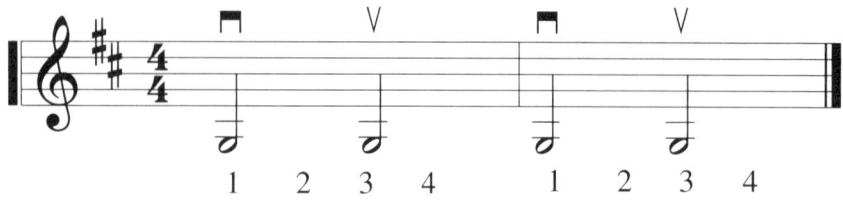

QUARTER NOTES

 12:50

EXERCISE 8

Now for short bow strokes. Place the bow on the 3rd string (D string), just above the middle, draw it out about 5 or 6 inches, and back again without stopping, one count for each bow stroke. These are called quarter notes.

♩ = Quarter note

EXERCISE 9

Now, the same technique on the 2nd string (A string).

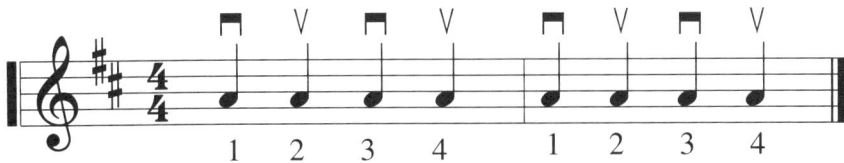

EXERCISE 10

To the first string (E string).

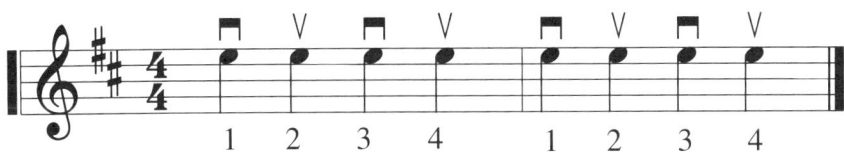

EXERCISE 11

Now the 4th string.

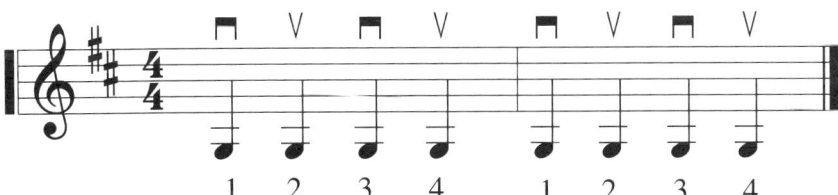

There are two primary factors that contribute to good tone and bowing on the violin, bow speed and bow pressure. Practice varying these two factors to get a pleasing tone. Too slow with too much pressure produces the horrible grinding sound. Too fast makes a breathy indistinct sound. Too close to the bridge makes a whistling sound.

OPEN STRING EXERCISES

In the following exercises, we will use quarter notes, half notes, and whole notes and swap back and forth from the D string (3rd string) to the A string (2nd string). Play along with the CD to make sure you are playing each exercise correctly.

EXERCISE 12

EXERCISE 13

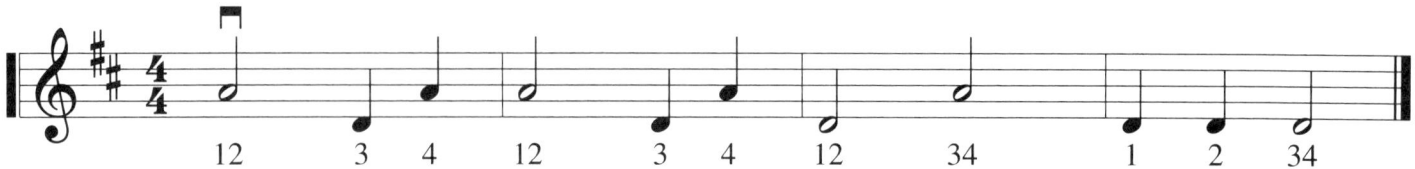

EXERCISE 14

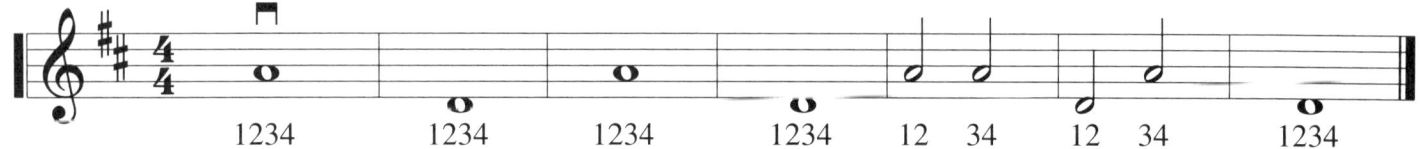

EXERCISE 15

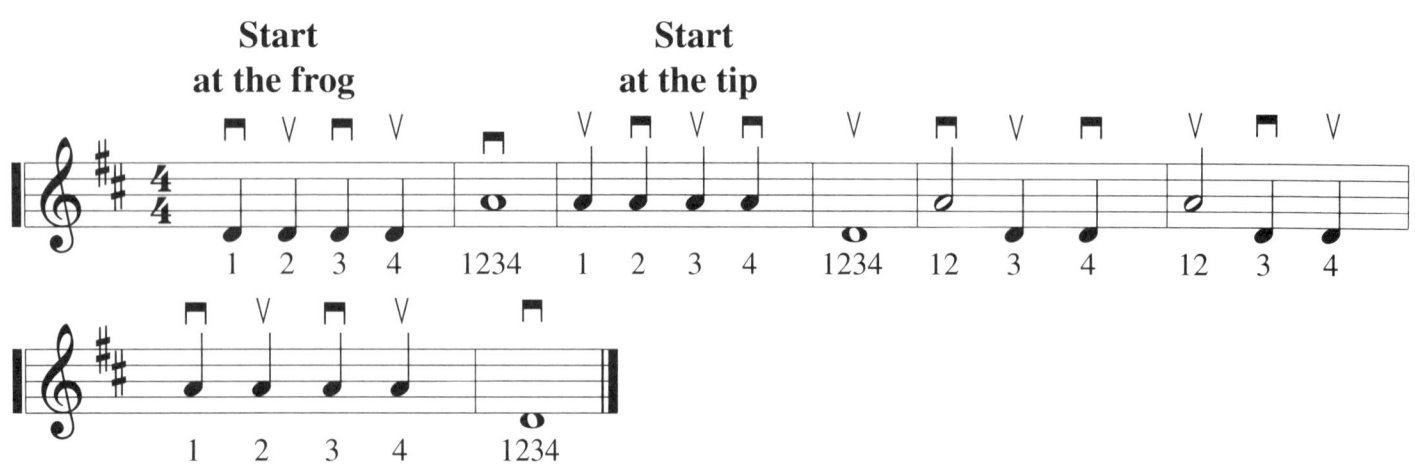

 **EXERCISE 16**

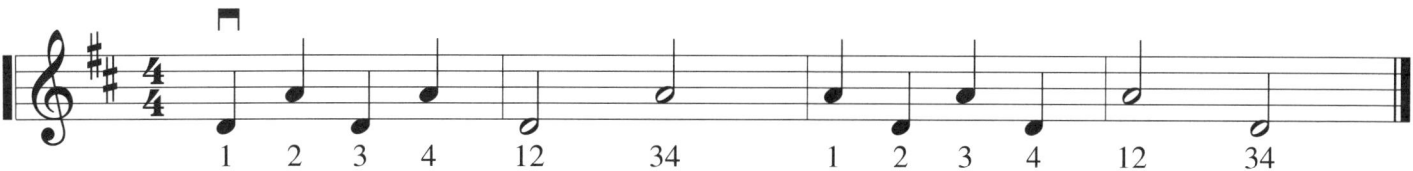

 **EXERCISE 17**

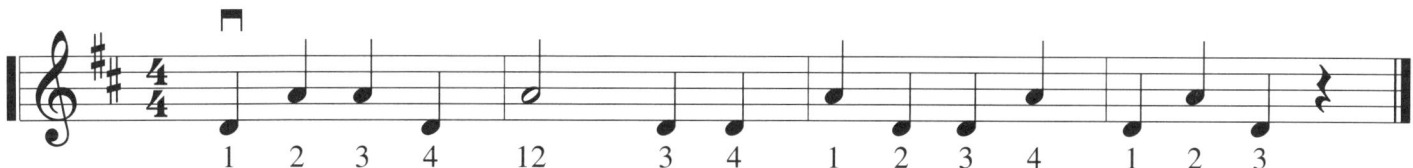

Play all of these exercises several times until you are comfortable with all of them. Make sure you play along with the CD.

NOTING THE VIOLIN

Now we'll start using the left hand to press down the strings in order to play different notes. Review the left hand and wrist positions we covered earlier.

EXERCISE 19

With your index finger (first finger), press down on the 3rd string about 1 1/8 inches from the nut. Place the bow on the 3rd string a little closer to the frog than the middle. Bow down on the open D string, then up, noting E with your index finger. What you are doing is playing the 1st & 2nd notes of a D major scale. Bow down and up, making small adjustments until you can match this pitch, neither too high or too low. Listen to the CD or video tape.

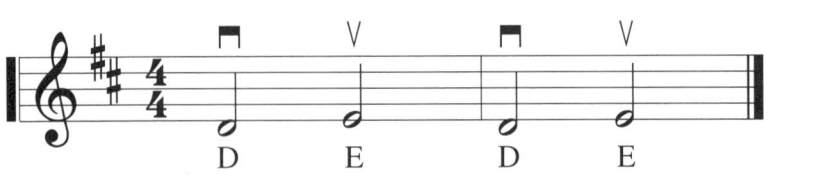

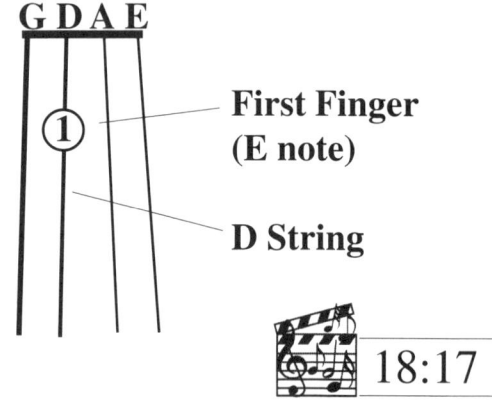

 EXERCISE 20

18:17

Below you will see two measures that we will repeat many times. First D, played for a half note, 2 beats, on the down bow, then E, a half note, on the up bow for a total of 2 beats. I'll play the 1st measure and you play the 2nd measure. We'll call these answer backs. Play along with the CD or video tape.

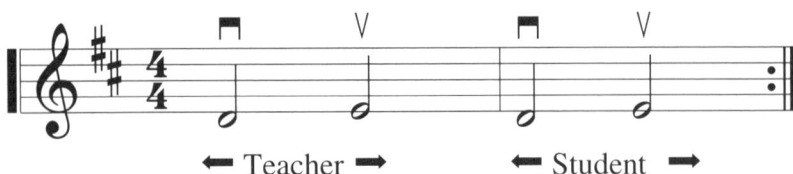

The goal of this exercise is to learn just where that note is, both with your ears and it's location on the fingerboard. Rewind the video or the CD and answer back many times. Make sure you are in tune with the CD and match the pitch exactly. It will take some practice.

 EXERCISE 21  19:15

Next we'll learn the F# note. It's noted with the 2nd finger, about another inch or so up the fingerboard from the 1st finger. What we are doing is constructing the distance from the 1st note to the 3rd note of a major scale. It's location on the staff is in the bottom space. We'll put the sharp in the key signature on the left hand side of the staff, indicating that all F's, including the one in the bottom space, are sharp.

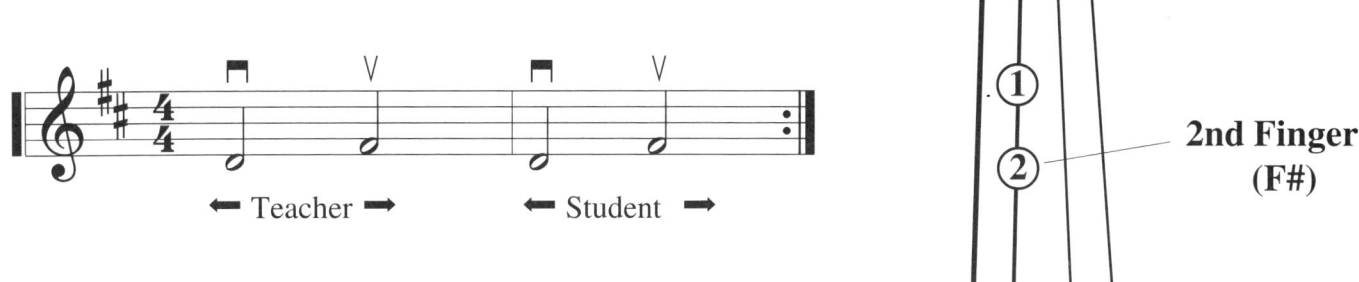

If your F# is too high (sharp) or too low (flat), don't stop the bow. Continue to play smoothly and make a correction, up or down, on the next answer back.

 EXERCISE 22

Now we'll do another set of answer backs that should make it even easier to find these notes. This exercise will include A, the open 2nd string, located on the staff in the next to bottom space. Bow the open D, then E with your index finger, then the open A, then back to the E with your index finger. This will give you 2 points of reference for pitch, the D & A strings, and two opportunities to make those little corrections. Check your bow grip and we're off.

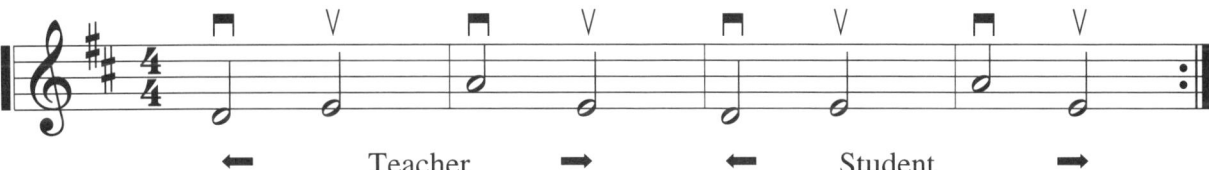

 EXERCISE 23

Now the same with the 2nd finger on F#. First open D, then F#, open A (the second string), and back to F#.

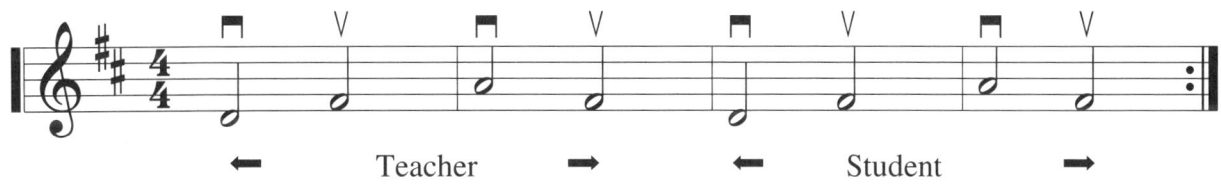

21

This section of the book could well prove invaluable to you as your ear improves. What may have sounded in tune the first few days might seem questionable as your ear gets a better idea of just where these notes are. This is all a normal part of improvement.

EXERCISE 24

Let's walk up the fingerboard using our 3 notes, D, E, & F#. Open D, 1st finger, 2nd finger

 # OUR FIRST SONG

We're just about ready to play a tune. First we'll divide the song into exercises before we try to put it all together. Play along with the CD or video tape.

EXERCISE 25

EXERCISE 26

EXERCISE 27

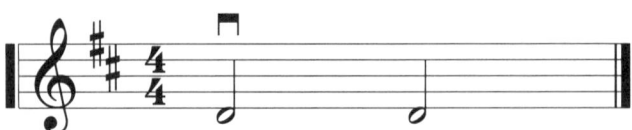

Playing small parts, especially the difficult or unfamiliar parts, helps insure success when you finally dive in to play the whole piece.

HERE WE GO

You should practice this song over and over, playing along with the video or CD, until you feel comfortable with it and can play it correctly.

 # MARY HAD A LITTLE LAMB

Frequently it helps beginners to play pieces they know, songs they hear in their head, or can sing. Our next piece is Mary Had A Little Lamb, a song virtually everyone is familiar with. Again, we will divide it in to exercises.

EXERCISE 28

EXERCISE 29

EXERCISE 30

EXERCISE 31

Now for the complete song.

 # MARY HAD A LITTLE LAMB

 **EXERCISE 32**

Practice the following exercises, playing along with the CD.

 **EXERCISE 33**

 EXERCISE 34  28:30

We're ready to learn three new notes, G, A, & B. The first is G. It's located on the next to bottom line. It is noted with the third finger (ring finger), but instead of being another inch or so up the fingerboard, it is right next to the second finger. On most people's hands the 2nd & 3rd fingers will touch or very nearly touch. Let's walk up to this note using the notes we already know, D, E, F#, and then G.

 EXERCISE 35

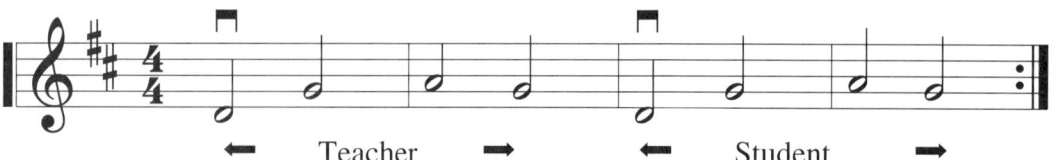

 EXERCISE 36

Let's add the open A string to our row of notes, D, E, F#, & G to play the first five notes of a major scale, both up and down.

 EXERCISE 37

We've got five notes in a row and now here comes the sixth. It's B, the note played with the first finger on the A string, the 2nd string. It's as far up the A string as the E was up the D string. It's location on the staff is on the middle line. Let's do some answer backs, A to B in half notes.

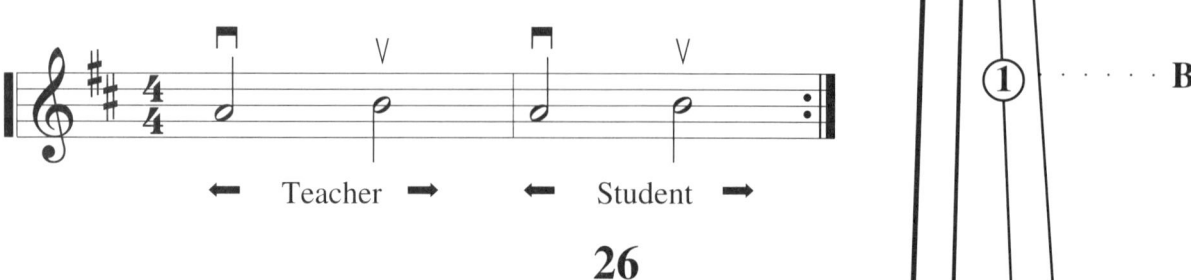

At this point we've got enough notes to play the Alphabet song. Let's divide it up into exercises.

EXERCISE 38

EXERCISE 39

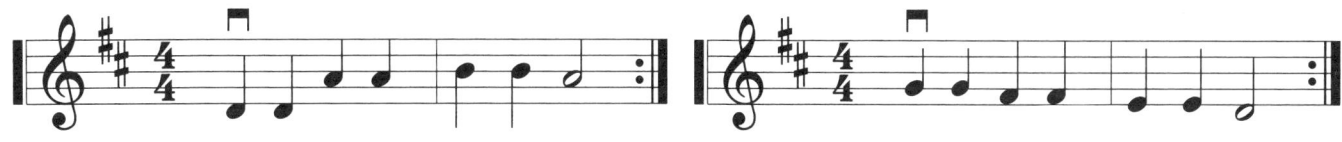

EXERCISE 40

Now we'll put the whole song together

THE ALPHABET SONG

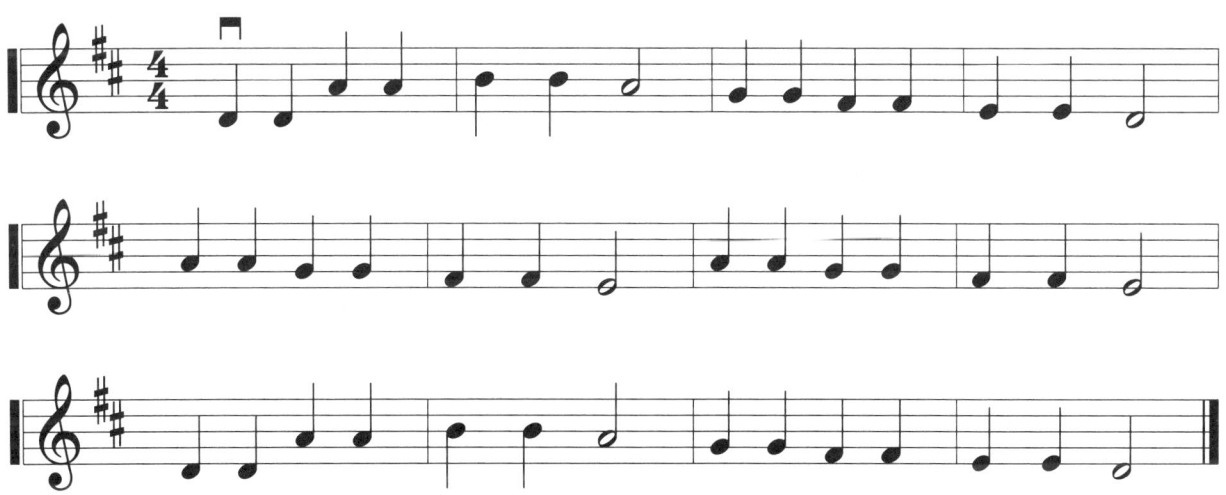

 **EXERCISE 41**

The next two exercises are in the key of G. The tonal center (the final note) is now G. Play along with the CD.

 **EXERCISE 42**

PRACTICE

The most important part of learning to play the violin is to develop consistent and efficient practice habits. The beginning student must have patience because playing the violin requires training the hands to do movements they have never done before and to strengthen muscles not normally used. You should average 30 minutes of practice each day. With consistent practice you should be comfortable with the violin and be able to play a few songs slowly within 4 - 6 weeks. Once you learn to play a few things on the violin, you'll find the learning process comes easier and your progress will start to snowball.

Following are some helpful hints and pointers concerning practice:

1. Go over your lesson assignment EVERY day. On days that it seems impossible to practice, make yourself go over the lesson for 4 or 5 minutes to reinforce things.
2. Practice 30 minutes a day if you are a beginner and divide this time into 10 or 15 minute segments. It has been proven that the human mind cannot concentrate heavily for more than 15 minutes.
3. Set up practice times to coincide with other activities such as when you wake up, when you go to bed, or when you come home at the end of the day. 15 minutes in the morning and 15 minutes at night works well for many people.
4. If possible set up a special practice area. Buy an inexpensive music stand and keep your lessons on it so you can start to work immediately with each practice session.
5. Avoid marathon 2 or 3 hour practice sessions on the weekends. The mind can only concentrate for short periods and most marathon sessions accomplish about the same amount of learning as a 15 minute practice session. In addition, many students use the "Marathon Practice Session" as an excuse to not practice every day.
6. Learn to identify and focus on the hard parts of each song. Put your efforts there as opposed to playing a song from start to finish over and over. Some techniques and movements require several hundred repetitions over several weeks while others are learned immediately after an few tries.
7. Practice the violin at first by looking in a mirror to make sure you are using the proper position.
8. Relax - if frustrated with a particular measure or technique, go to another or just take a break and come back after you feel better.
9. Ask your teacher or a friend to let you know how you are doing every couple of weeks. It is very encouraging because they notice your progress even though you think you are standing still. It's the same thing that happened when you were little and hadn't seen your cousins for a couple of years and were amazed by how much they had grown. They did not notice the growth because it was so gradual on a daily basis.
10. Record and listen to your own playing. This will help you locate areas that need work and also measure progress. Your tapes will improve as you practice more and more.
11. Remember always - Violin playing is a lot of fun no matter what your level of competence. Relax and enjoy yourself.

SECTION II
SONGS

SLURS

For our next song, we're going to learn a new bowing technique. It's called slurring or playing two or more notes on a bow stroke.

EXERCISE 43

Draw a down bow on the 3rd string (D string) for one beat of D, then finger the E note with the index finger for one beat, all without stopping the bow. Continue with the up bow on open D for the 3rd beat, and finger the E with the index finger on the 4th beat. Here's what it looks like written out.

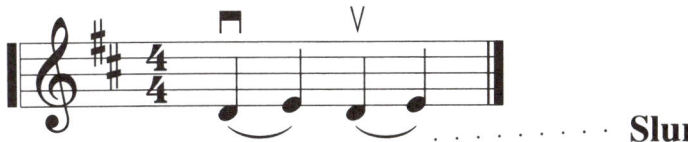
.... **Slur**

The curved line connecting the D to the E is the slur. In violin music, it means to play all the notes connected by that bow on either one up bow or one down bow. Let's get started on this with just two notes per bow and we'll do it in the form of answer backs. I'll play four beats, you play four beats.

It'll probably feel a little awkward, like patting your head and rubbing your stomach, because you're used to changing notes with the left hand as you change bow directions. Just practice slowly until you get more comfortable with it.

EXERCISE 44

There are other possibilities with slurring and we'll do them all in answer backs. First, notes going down, in this case, F# to E.

31

 EXERCISE 45

Another possibility could be slurring notes that are further apart than two adjacent notes in the scale, in this case, E to G, 1st finger to 3rd finger.

 EXERCISE 46

And last, before we play our song, the possibility of going from one string to another, all on the same bow stroke. Here, A to G. Open A to G, with the 3rd finger on the D string. Let's try it.

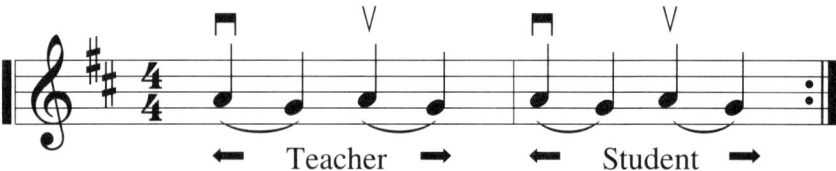

We'll break the song down into exercises first.

 EXERCISE 47

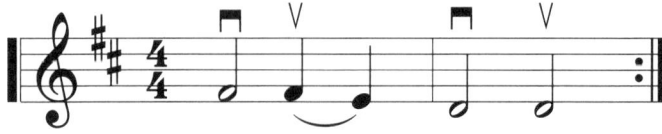

 EXERCISE 48

 **EXERCISE 49**

 **EXERCISE 50**

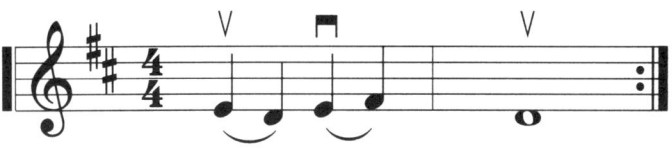

 # GO TELL AUNT RHODY

Play along with the video or CD many times until you feel comfortable with slurs.

 EXERCISE 51

Here are some more exercises for practicing slurs. Play smoothly and connect the notes.

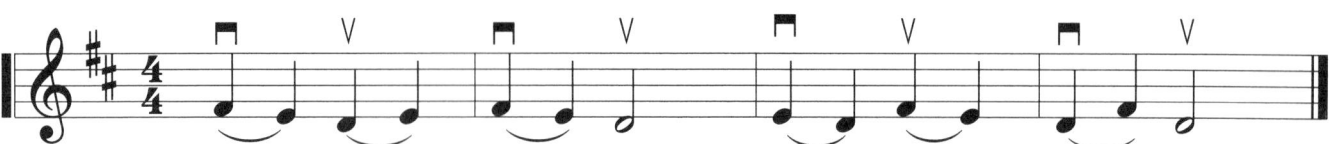

 EXERCISE 52

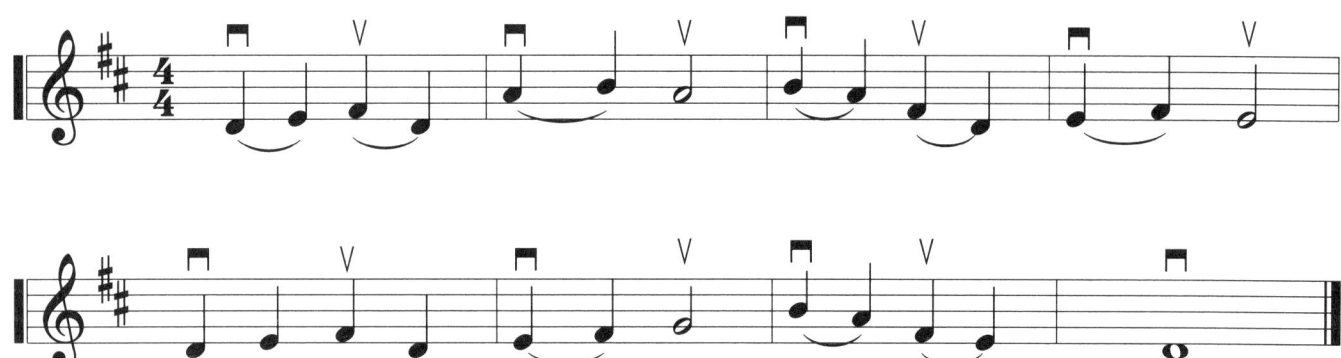

EXERCISE 53

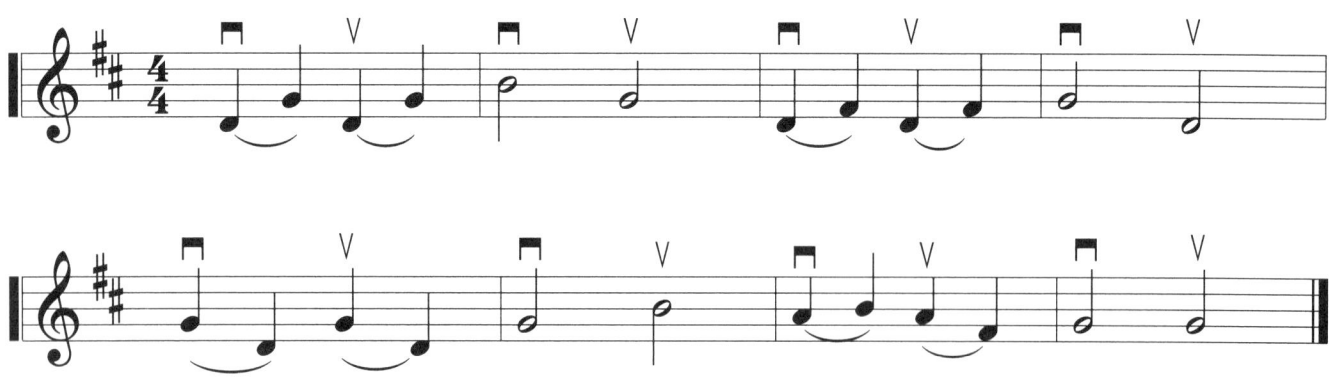

THE D SCALE

Let's learn two more notes. They'll be C# & D on the A string.

EXERCISE 54

On the staff, C# is found on the next to top space, and the key signature tells us that it's sharp, and D is the next to top line. They are noted with the second and third fingers of the left hand respectively. C# is an inch or so above the B with the second finger. D is located just above the C# with the third finger touching or nearly touching the second finger. The distance between notes on the 2nd string follow the same pattern as the distance between notes on the 3rd string. Let's accustom ourselves to these new notes with some answer backs. First A to C#.

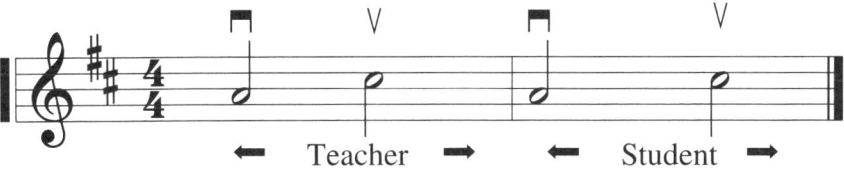

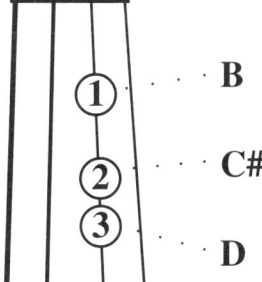

 ## EXERCISE 55

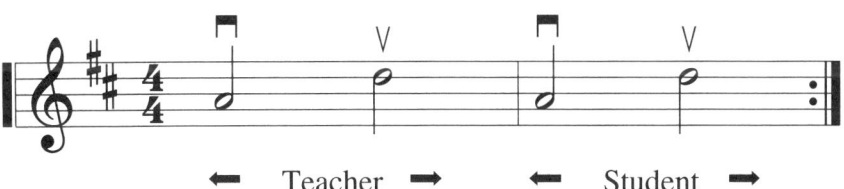

 ## EXERCISE 56

Here are some two string answer backs using the open first string or E string. The note sounded by the first string is found on the top space.

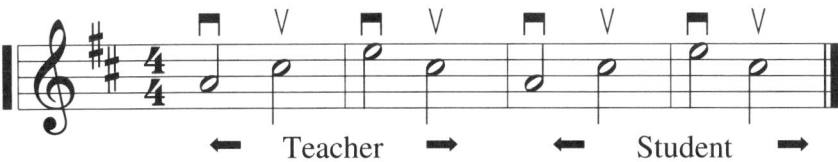

35

 # EXERCISE 57

 # EXERCISE 58

We now have enough notes to complete a D major scale. Here it is in half notes.

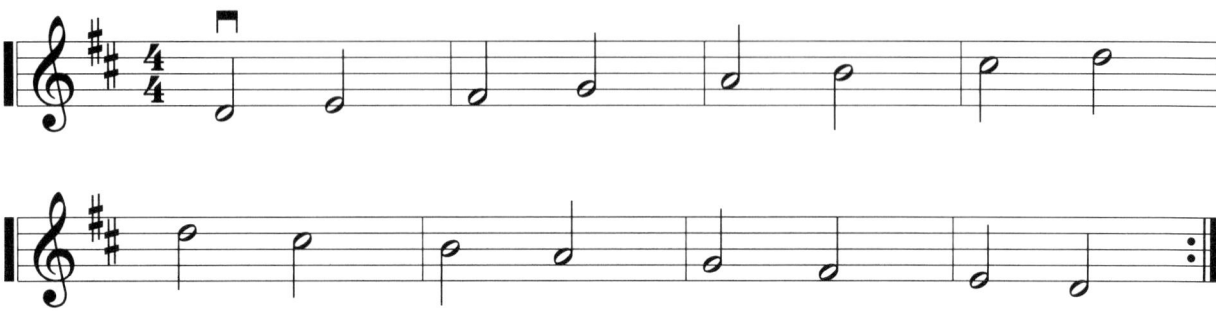

EXERCISE 59

Now we'll play it a little faster, using quarter notes

 # EXERCISE 60

To build your sense of tonality, also play arpeggios. An arpeggio is a chord, only with the notes sounded one at a time. Our D arpeggio will have D, F#, A, and high D, both ascending and descending.

Do plenty of listening to the CD, because you are training your ears to hear how high or low these notes are as you are training your fingers to find the exact location. In this sense you can't play what you can't hear, so listen carefully and intently.

In Exercises 61 through 64, listen carefully to the distances or intervals between notes.

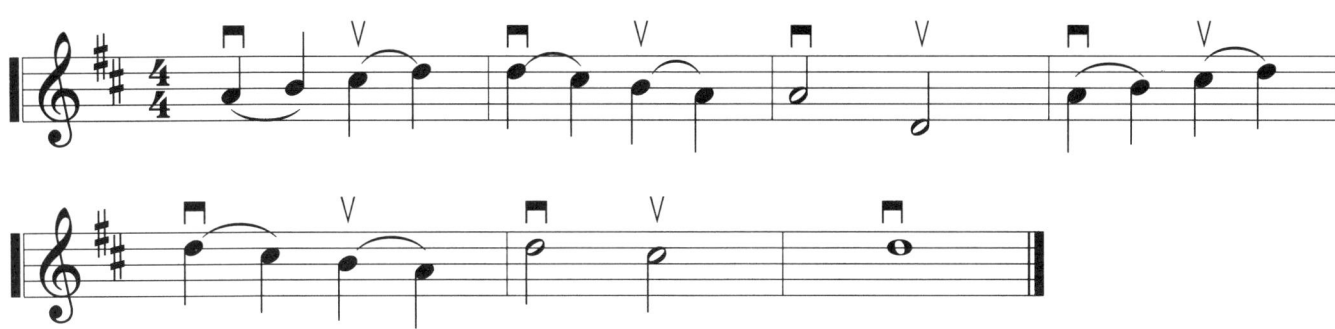

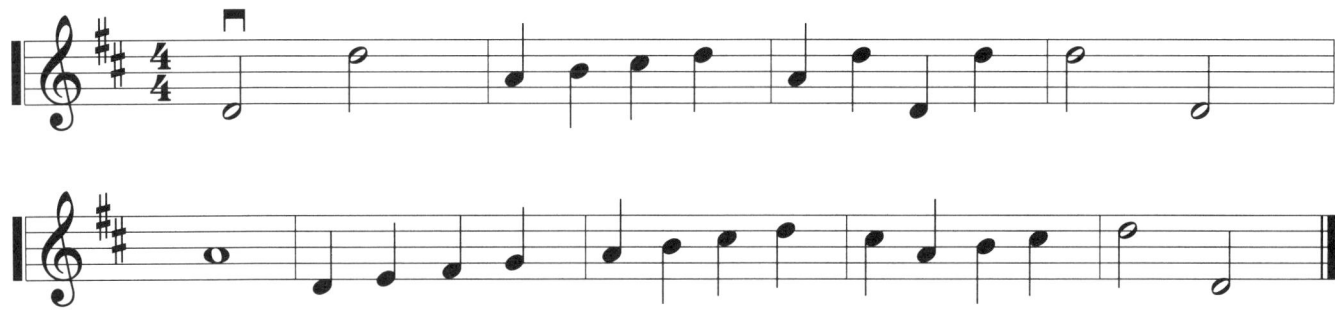

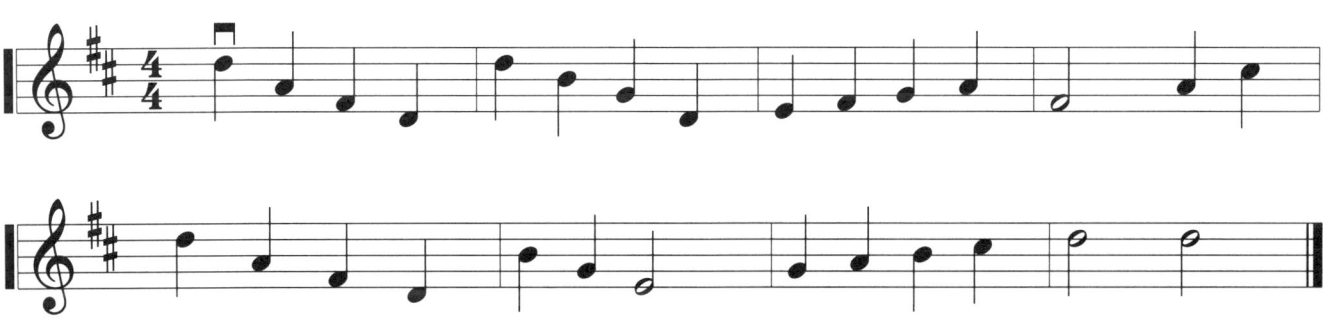

3/4 TIME

To play the next song, we'll need some new rhythmic concepts. First 3/4 time. If you recall, the top number in the time signature indicates the number of beats per measure, in this case, 3. The quarter note receives one beat as shown by the bottom number. 3/4 feels very different than 4/4. Instead of 1,2,3,4, it counts as 123,123. Notes that receive 3 beats are dotted half notes. The principle here is that a dot placed after a note increases it's time value by half, 2 beats increases to 3. In written music, rests indicate that you sound no note for a given duration.

EXERCISE 65

Let's practice playing in four bar segments, like this.

EXERCISE 66

Start the bow at the tip.

EXERCISE 67

Start with the bow at the tip and begin with an up bow.

EXERCISE 68

SUNDAY WALTZ

 **EXERCISE 69**

Here are some exercises using slurring in 3/4 time. Play along with the CD.

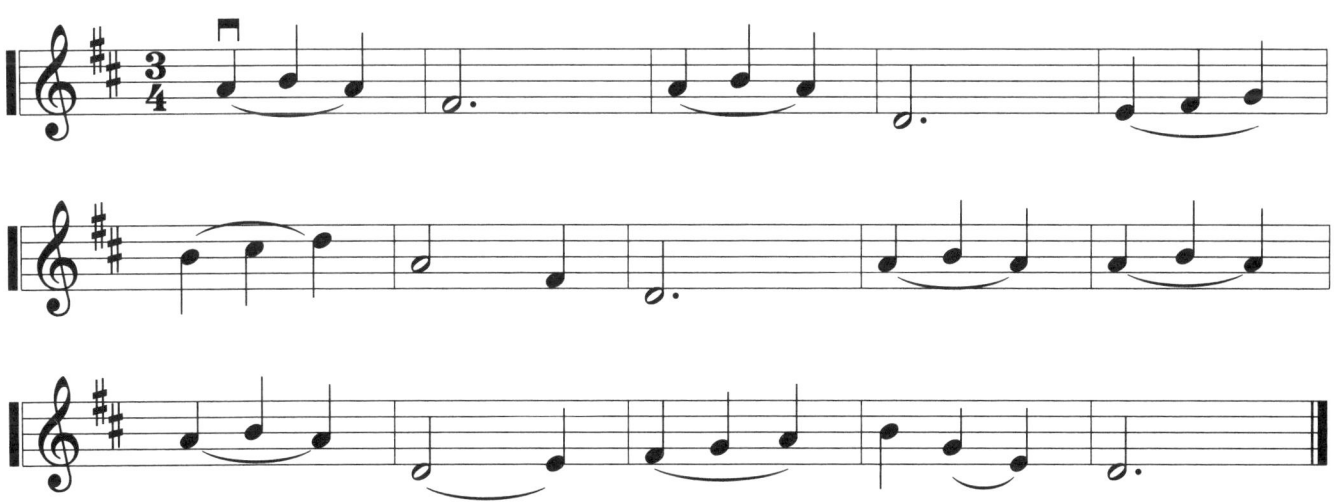

EXERCISE 70

C NATURAL

C natural is played with the 2nd finger on the A string. Place it close to the first finger. Play along with the CD for the following answer backs.

EXERCISE 71

EXERCISE 72

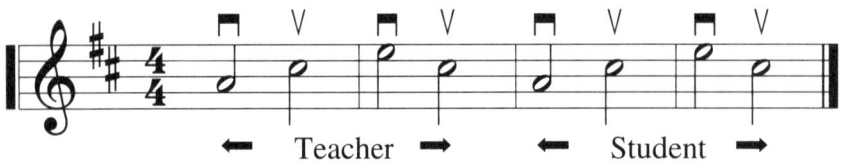

 EXERCISE 73

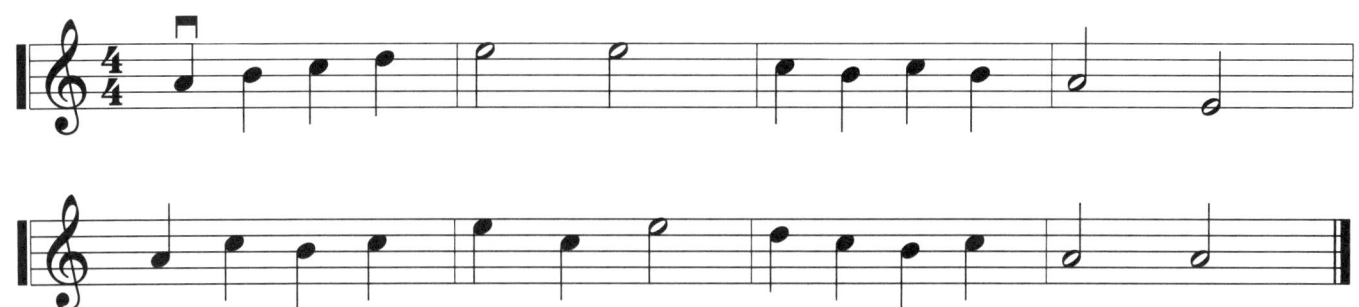

Here's an old English dance tune. Violinists have been playing this song for dancers for centuries.

JENNY PLUCK PEARS

 EXERCISE 74

Pay special attention to measures 3 & 7. The second finger will be low on the C natural on the A string and high on the F# on the D string.

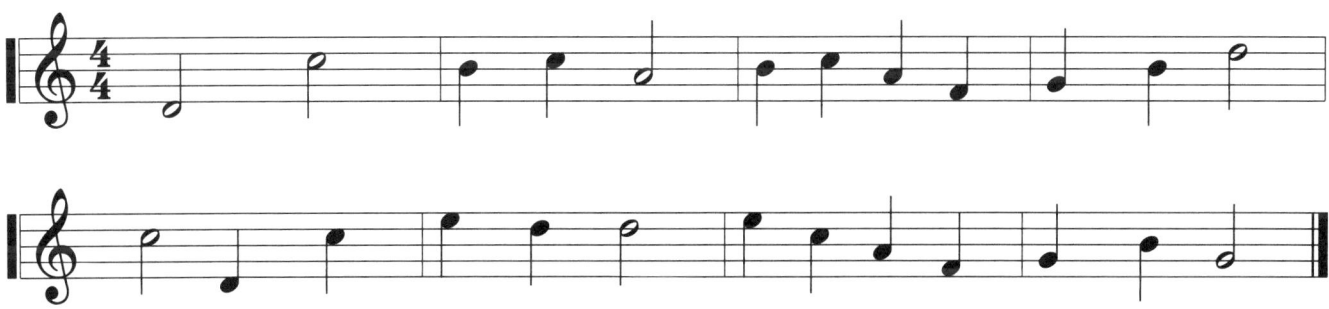

TIES

When two notes of the same pitch are connected by a curved line, it is called a tie. Play the total number of beats in both notes on one bow stroke. Ties may cross bar lines.

EXERCISE 75

Play along with the CD.

EXERCISE 76

In this song, place the bow on the string at the tip and start with an up bow.

WHEN THE SAINTS GO MARCHING IN

RED RIVER VALLEY

NEW NOTES ON THE E STRING

The notes we'll play on the E string (1st string) are the open E, F#, G, and A. We'll play the F# first. It's played with the first finger about as far up the string as on the D and A strings. It's location on the staff is on the top line.

EXERCISE 77

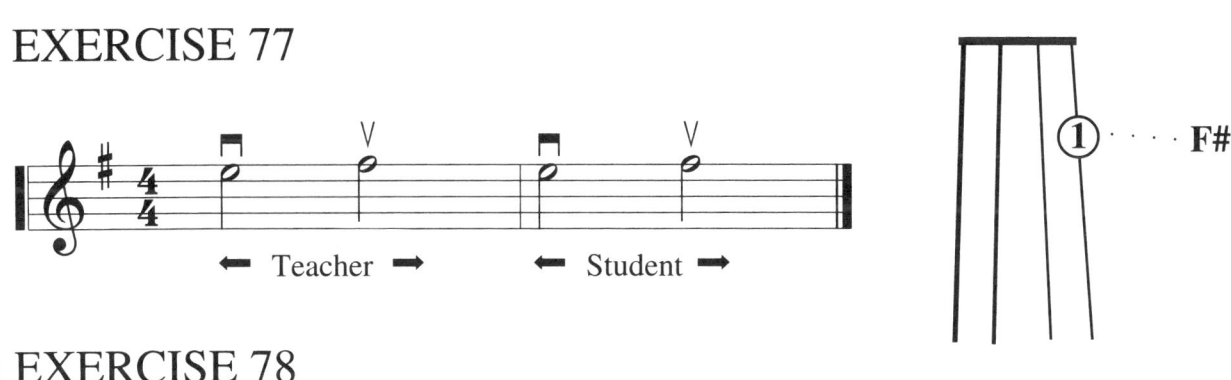

EXERCISE 78

Here's a two string answer back with a lower open string for reference.

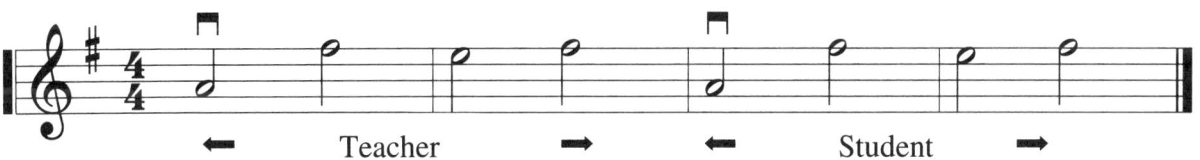

EXERCISE 79

EXERCISE 80

G natural is found on the space above the top line. It's played with the second finger close to the F# note.

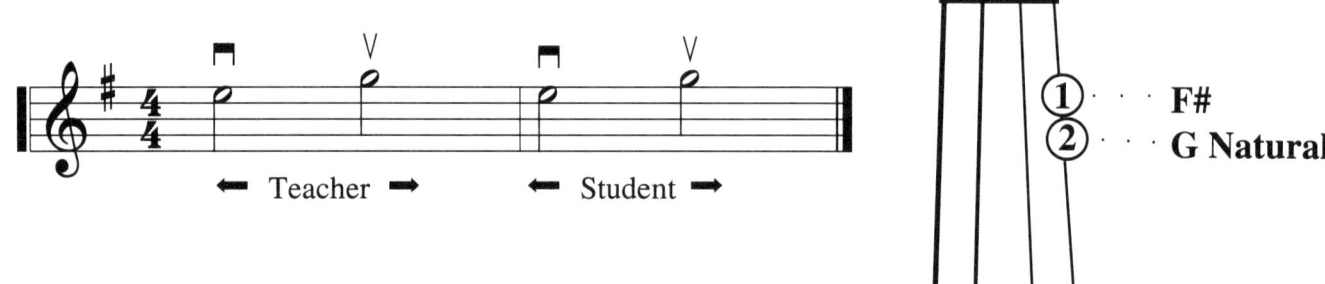

EXERCISE 81

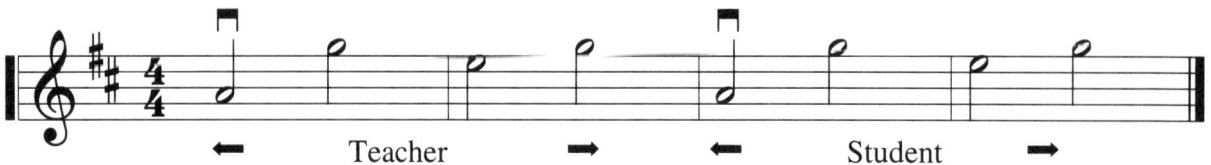

EXERCISE 82

# EXERCISE 83

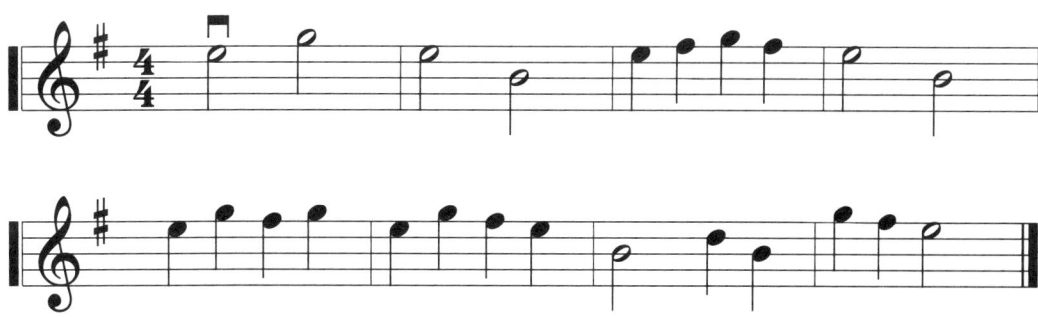

# EXERCISE 84

Now we have the notes we need to play the G major scale.

# EXERCISE 85

The A note is located on the first ledger line above the staff. It is played with the 3rd finger.

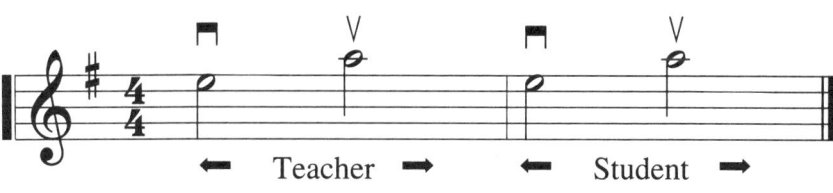
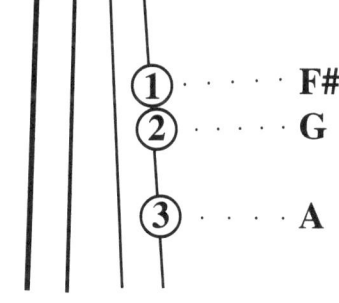

# EXERCISE 86

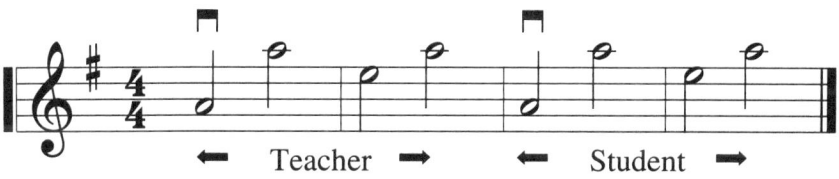

EXERCISE 87

EXERCISE 88

Here are the first five notes of the D major scale played an octave higher.

Begin on the up bow. Take care with the jump from high A to the A an octave lower.

SEAGULLS AND SEALS

SWEET ON VIOLIN

MUSIC THEORY

To become an accomplished violinist you must understand some basic principals about the violin and music in general so that you can get the overall picture of the music you are playing.

A major scale consists of 7 notes, which we will number 1-7.

Notes In Major Scales

Scale		1	2	3	4	5	6	7
Key of C		C	D	E	F	G	A	B
Key of G	(1#)	G	A	B	C	D	E	F#
Key of D	(2#)	D	E	F#	G	A	B	C#
Key of A	(3#)	A	B	C#	D	E	F#	G#
Key of E	(4#)	E	F#	G#	A	B	C#	D#
Key of F	(1b)	F	G	A	Bb	C	D	E
Key of Bb	(2b)	Bb	C	D	Eb	F	G	A
Key of Eb	(3b)	Eb	F	G	Ab	Bb	C	D
Key of Ab	(4b)	Ab	Bb	C	Db	Eb	F	G

A **chromatic scale** consists of 12 notes, all the notes possible to play in one octave. All of the notes are shown below. The notes on top of each other are identical. For instance, the A# and the Bb are the same. These are called **Enharmonic Tones**.

Chromatic Scale

1	2	3	4	5	6	7	8	9	10	11	12
A	A#	B	C	C#	D	D#	E	F	F#	G	G#
	Bb			Db		Eb			Gb		Ab

Notice that there is no note between B & C, and no note between E & F. A **half step** is one note in the chromatic scale (A to A# is a half step). A **whole step** is two notes in the chromatic scale (A to B is a whole step).

To figure out the notes in any major scale, use the following guides:

Notes	1		2		3		4		5		6		7		1
		whole step		whole step		half step		whole step		whole step		whole step		half step	

For example, to figure out the notes in an A Scale, start with an A note in the chromatic scale. To go to note 2 make a whole step to B. Note 3 would be a whole step to C#. Note 4 is a half step to D. Note 5 is a whole step to E. Note 6 is a whole step to F#. Note 7 is a whole step to G#. Note 1 is a half step back to A.

CIRCLE OF 5THS

The circle of 5ths is useful for memorizing the order of sharps or flat keys, as well as the order in which the sharps or flats occur.

Beginning with the key of C and moving clockwise in steps of 5ths, each key has one more sharp than the one before it. Moving counterclockwise from C in steps of 4ths, each key has one more flat than the one before it.

Each new sharp is the 7th of the key in which it occurs. Each new flat is the 4th of the key in which it occurs.

The key signatures as they would appear in music notation are shown inside the circle. To figure out the name of the flat keys from the key signature, use the next to last flat. Move the last sharp up one note (1/2 step or 1 fret) to figure out the name of the sharp keys.

Notice that there are 12 different major keys, but three of them have different names. Keys that have the same key signature, but have different names are called Enharmonic keys.

The relative minor key of each major key, which is the 6th of that key, is shown inside the circle. The relative minor has the same key signature as its relative major key.

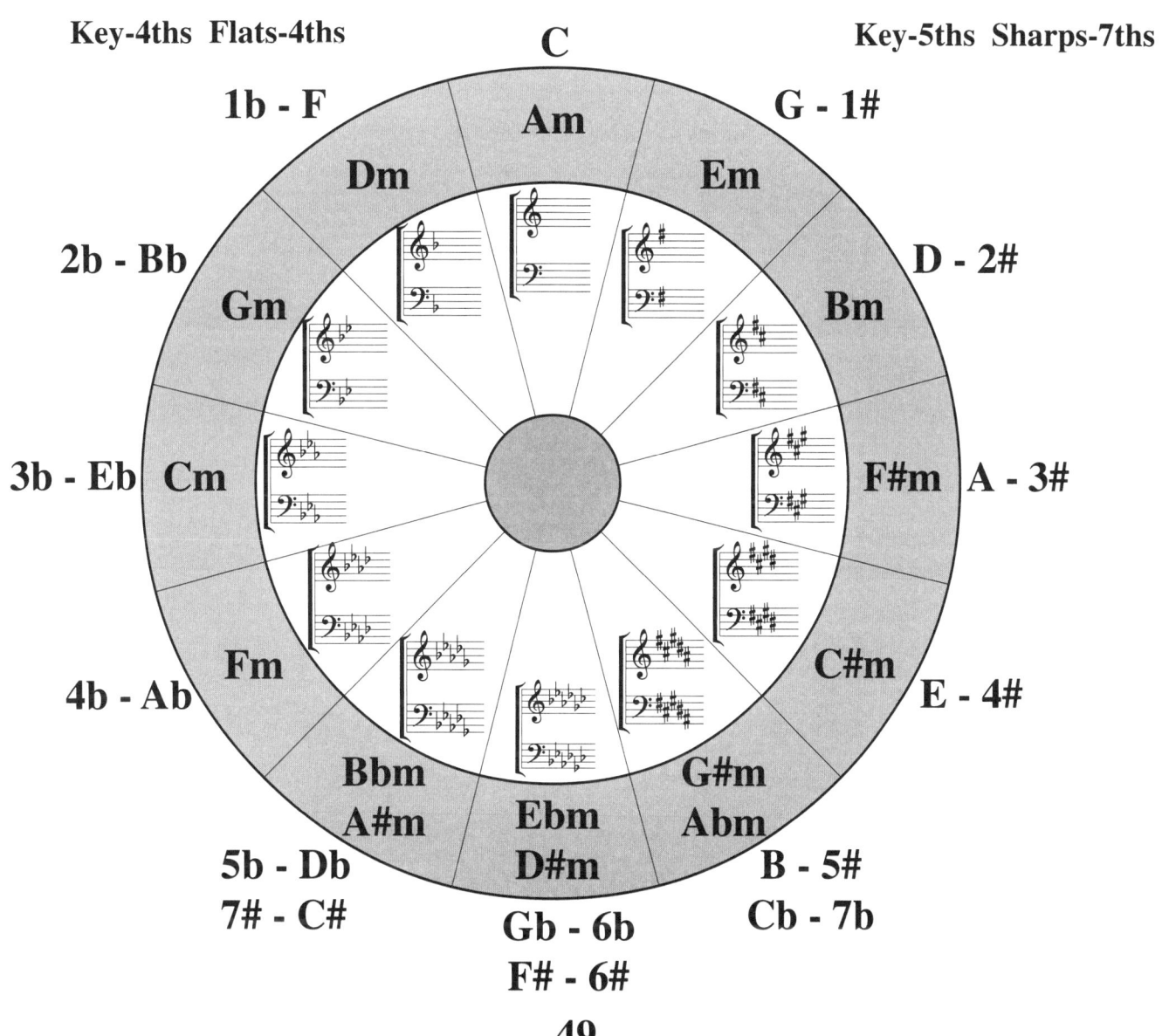

Notes